BIBLE KEY WORDS

VIII. LORD

MANUALS FROM KITTEL

BIBLE KEY WORDS
FROM GERHARD KITTEL'S
THEOLOGISCHES WÖRTERBUCH
ƵUM NEUEN TESTAMENT

LORD

BY

WERNER FOERSTER

AND

GOTTFRIED QUELL

ADAM & CHARLES BLACK
LONDON

THIS EDITION FIRST PUBLISHED 1958
BY A. AND C. BLACK LIMITED
4, 5 AND 6 SOHO SQUARE LONDON W.1

Translated from the German
first edition, Stuttgart, 1933,
and with additional notes,
by H. P. Kingdon

MADE IN GREAT BRITAIN
PRINTED AT THE UNIVERSITY PRESS
ABERDEEN

TRANSLATOR'S PREFACE

THIS volume is a translation of the article in Kittel's New Testament *Wörterbuch* entitled *Kurios*—the Greek word used in the Septuagint for the Hebrew *Yahweh* as well as the periphrase for the name of God, *'ādhôn*, " lord ". Thus the article is concerned not only with the root meanings of the word *kurios* in classical Greek, but just as much with the Old Testament *Yahweh* or Jehovah, and also with similar terms used of God in Syria and Egypt which came to be rendered as *kurios* in Greek. In fact it is maintained that the basic meaning of *kurios*—a lord who commands willing service—owes much to this oriental background.

Many more quotations have been left in the original Greek than in the companion volume on *Basileia*, as the contentions here advanced demanded a greater wealth of detailed evidence in their support. But here too a few of the key Greek words have been transliterated, as well as all the Hebrew terms, in order to help non-specialists pick up the main thread of the argument. It should be obvious that, e.g. *rhabbi* is a transliteration of the Greek, *rabbî* of the Hebrew form of the word meaning " teacher ", which the German text prints in Greek or Hebrew letters respectively.

The expression " op. cit." refers to books listed in the Bibliography as well as to earlier references in the text or footnotes. Less than one-tenth of the detailed citations in the German text have been omitted, the most important of these omissions being indicated, usually by printing dots in the translation. All the other few additions I have made are printed in square brackets. In the transliteration of the Hebrew in this volume, invaluable help has been given by the Rev. Islwyn Blythin, tutor at Didsbury College and

Recognised Teacher in Hebrew and Religious Knowledge at Bristol University.

Of the two authors of the original German, Professor Quell of Rostock is mentioned in the prefaces to the volumes in this series entitled *Love* and *Sin*. It may be added that in 1952 he published a monograph on *Wahre und falsche Propheten*. Professor Foerster was born in 1897 and has spent most of his life teaching in Münster. Besides the book mentioned in the Bibliography, and the articles he has contributed to the *Wörterbuch* (for which he is also working on the subject *christos*), he is the author of works on Gnosticism and of two volumes on *Neutestamentliche Zeitgeschichte* (1940 and 1956), and he brought out a *Kurzgefasste Bibelkunde des N.T.* in 1952. He has kindly contributed several of my additions to the original Bibliography. My thanks are due to him and also to Professor G. Friedrich of Erlangen, Kittel's successor as Editor of the *Wörterbuch*.

H. P. KINGDON

CONTENTS

SELECT BIBLIOGRAPHY

W. Bousset : *Kyrios Christos*, 2nd edn. (1921).

A. Deissmann : *Licht vom Osten*, 4th edn. (1923).

H. Lietzmann : *Kommentar zum Römerbrief*, 3rd edn. (1928).

H. Cremer : *Bibl.-theol. Wörterbuch. d.N.T. Gr.*, 11th edn., revised by J. Kögel (1923), pp. 644-55.

E. Rohde in *Z.N.W.*, xxii (1923), pp. 43 ff.

K. Prümm : *Herrscherkult und N.T.*, in *Biblica*, ix (1928), pp. 1 ff.

W. W. Graf Baudissin : *Kyrios als Gottesname* . . . (1929).

I. A. Smith in *J.T.S.*, xxxi (1930), pp. 155-60.

A. D. Nock in *Essays on the Trinity and Incarnation*, ed. A. E. J. Rawlinson (1928), pp. 51 ff.

C. H. Dodd : *The Bible and the Greeks* (1935), pp. 8-11.

[K. Prümm : *Der christliche Glaube und die heidnische Welt*, i, (1935), 214-25.]

Further literature in W. Foerster, *Herr ist Jesus* (1924), pp. 11-56.

CHAPTER I

K. Stegmann von Pritzwald : *Zur Geschichte der Herrscherbezeichnungen von Homeros bis Platon* (1930), §§86, 110, 155.

[K. Prümm : *Religionsgeschichtliches Handbuch für den Raum der altchristlichen Welt*, 2nd edn. (1954), s.v. ' Herrscherkult '.]

CHAPTER II

W. Drexler, in Roscher's *Lexikon der griechischen und römischen Mythologie*, s.v.

O. Eissfeldt : *Götternamen und Gottesvorstellung bei den Semiten*, in *Zeitschrift der Deutschen Morgenländischen Gesellschaft* (1929), pp. 21-36.

CHAPTER III

A. Alt : *Jahwe*, in *Reallexikon der Vorgeschichte*, vi (1926), 147 ff.

W. R. Arnold : " The Divine Name " in *Journal of Biblical Literature*, xxiv (1905), 107 ff.

M. Buber : *Königtum Gottes*, 2nd edn. (1936).

M. Buber-F. Rosenzweig : *Die Schrift und ihre Verdeutschung* (1936), pp. 184 ff., 332 ff.

O. Grether : *Name und Wort Gottes im A.T.* (1934).

C. Toussaint : *Les Origines de la religion d'Israel*, vol. i, *L'ancien Jahvisme* (1931).

[G. R. Driver : " The Original Form of the name Yahweh : Evidence and Conclusion " in *Z.A.W.* (1928).]

Chapter IV

G. Dalman : *Worte Jesu*, 2nd edn. (1930), pp. 266-80.

G. F. Moore : *Judaism*, i (1927), 423 ff.

Strack-Billerbeck : Kommentar zum N.T. aus Talmud und Midrasch, vol. iii, p. 672, on Heb. 1, 2.

A. Marmorstein : *The Old Rabbinic Doctrine of God*, vol. i (1927), *The Names and Attributes of God*.

Chapter V

H. Weinel : *N.T. Theologie* (1928).

P. Feine : *N.T. Theologie* (1934), pp. 104 f., 175; [8th edn. (1951). pp. 30-3, 165 f.]

E. von Dobschütz : *Z.N.W.*, xxx (1931), 97-123.

E. Lohmeyer in *Z.N.W.*, xxvi (1927), 164-9.

F. H. Stead : "The chief Pauline names for Christ", The Expositor, III, Series 7 (1888), pp. 386-95.

E. W. Burton : *Galatians* (I.C.C.), pp. 393, 399-404.

K. Holl : *Gesammelte Aufsätze*, ii (1928), 115-22.

W. Schmauch : *In Christus* (1935).

[R. Bultmann : *N.T. Theologie*, pp. 52 f., 123-27.

M. Meinertz : *N.T. Theologie*, vol. i, p. 216 f., vol. ii, pp. 70-2.

O. Cullman : "Kyrios as a designation for the oral tradition concerning Jesus", in the *Scottish Journal of Theology*, 1950, pp. 180-97.

L. Cerfaux : "Kyrios dans les citations Pauliniennes de l'Ancient Testament" in *Ephemerides Lovanienses*, xx (1943), 5-17.

F. C. Grant : *An Introduction to New Testament Thought* (1950), pp. 130-7.

A. E. J. Rawlinson : *The New Testament Doctrine of the Christ* (1926), pp. 231-7.

E. Schweitzer : *Erniedrigung und Erhöhung bei Jesus und seinen Nachfolgern* (1955), esp. pp. 93 ff.]

ABBREVIATIONS

B.G.U.	Aegyptische Urkunden aus den kgl Museen zu Berlin.
C.I.G.	Corpus Inscriptionum Graecarum.
Ditt.Or.	W. Dittenberger, Orientis Graecae Inscriptiones.
Ditt. Syll.	W. Dittenberger, Sylloge Inscriptionum Graecarum.
I.G.	Inscriptiones Graecae.
J.H.S.	Journal of Hellenic Studies.
J.T.S.	Journal of Theological Studies.
L.	Material found only in St. Luke's Gospel.
LXX	The Septuagint.
Oxyr. Pap.	The Oxyrhyncus Papyri.
par.	" and parallel passages ".
R.G.G.	Religion in Geschichte und Gegenwarth[2] (1927 ff.)
Str-B.	H. L. Strack und P. Billerbeck, Kommentar zum N.T. aus Talmud und Midrasch (1922-28).
v.l.	varia lectio.
Z.A.W.	Zeitschrift für die alttestamentliche Wissenschaft.
Z.N.W.	Zeitschrift für die neutestamentliche Wissenschaft.

INTRODUCTION

In German the word "Herr" (lord) is the most
common expression of a situation confined to the
personal sphere of human life, and indeed of a situation
which constitutes an important part of personality,
the circumstance that there is such a thing as the
exercise of personal power over men and things.
Moreover man, whether in the human sphere he is
himself the subject of this exercise of power (as lord),
or its object (as slave) is, in relation to God, its object.
In the concept of lordship two things are brought
together into an organic unity : the exercise of power
as such, and the *personal* quality of its exercise, which
passes beyond mere external compulsion into the legal
and moral sphere. The exercise of power as such
occurs also in non-human experience as the expression
of the ordering of what is most expedient (the strongest
animal as the leader). The decisive difference about
the exercise of power amongst men is that it is
legitimated not only by the inescapable presence of
expediency but by an element of law which goes
beyond what is merely natural and expedient, which
turns merely temporal possession into the moral
category of ownership, changes the momentary superiority of the stronger into the authority of the ruler,
and turns the superiority of parents over children
(which naturally demands their subjection), or the
power of the slave-owner over his slaves, into something
which calls for subservience and imposes responsibility.
It seems that in the course of human history, from the
earliest stages to be inferred from the history of language,
the realisation of a unique unity of the two elements
in lordship was a matter of gradual development;

and very varied attempts to comprehend it rightly confront us in the general spiritual and religious history of men. But in none of these is achieved the full understanding that the two elements in their complete form are destined to be organically inter-woven. This understanding is only arrived at where man sees God as the Creator over against him, who " places " him in the exercise of His absolute power, i.e. creates him, and, as Creator, is at the same time his supreme authority, to serve whom connotes not slavery but freedom—in the sphere of the biblical revelation. There a humanity which has flung off all mere subordination to its creator confronts Him who with the authority of the serving and forgiving love of God woos its willing subservience, and makes all lordship-relations new.

I. THE MEANING OF THE WORD *ΚΥΡΙΟΣ*

'Ο κύριος, substantivised adj. κύριος, itself derived from the noun τὸ κῦρος, comes from an indo-germanic root keu(ā), kū, meaning " to swell " (cf. κυέω, ἔγκυος, ἐγκύμων, κῦμα), hence also " to be strong "; κύριος is connected with the old Indian śūra (strong, brave, hero). τὸ κῦρος (since Aeschylus) means " strength ", " power ", " might ", cf. Aeschylus Suppl. 391: οὐκ ἔχουσιν κῦρος οὐδὲν ἀμφὶ σοῦ, also " cause ": Soph. El. 918 f.: ἡ δὲ νῦν ἴσως πολλῶν ὑπάρξει κῦρος ἡμέρα καλῶν.

(1) *The adjective κύριος*

Hence the adjective κύριος means " possessing might ", or " having the power of law ", " legal ", " valid ", " justified ", " appropriate ", " plenipotentiary "; also " important ", " decisive ", " paramount ". As adjective, κύριος occurs from the classical to the N.T. period, but not in the N.T. nor in late-Jewish literature. This is bound up with the fact that the Hebrew and Aramaic equivalent to the noun ὁ κύριος has no corresponding adjective.

(*a*) " possessing might " (strength, power): Pindar, *Olymp.* I. 104, δύναμιν κυριώτερον " higher in power ": cf. fr. 260 (ed. W. Christ, 1896) of Palamedes: ὄντα μὲν αὐτὸν κυριώτερον τοῦ 'Οδυσσέως εἰς σοφίας λόγον. See also *Isthm.* 5, 53: Ζεὺς ὁ πάντων κύριος; cf. Plutarch, *Def. Orac.* 29 (II, 426a): " if there are several worlds, does it follow that there are also several Zeuses, and not one, οἷος ὁ παρ' ἡμῖν κύριος ἀπάντων καὶ πατὴρ ἐπονομαζόμενος? [1] The

---

[1] In the Pindar quotation κύριος must be an adjective, in that from Plutarch it is more of a noun.

possession of physical strength is, by and large, not indicated by κύριος: the nearest passage to this is Plutarch, *Aristides* 6 (I, 322b): three emotions possess mankind *vis-à-vis* the divine, ζῆλος, φόβος, τιμή. . . . ἐκπλήττεσθαι δὲ καὶ δεδιέναι κατὰ τὸ κύριον καὶ δυνατόν. It is far more a question of *power of disposing or enacting:* cf. Demosthenes, *Or.* 50, 60 of the dying mother—οὐκέτι τῶν ὄντων κυρία οὖσα, 8, 69—a constitution, in which πλειόνων ἡ τύχη κυρία γίνεται ἢ οἱ λογισμοί: 18, 194: οὐ . . . τῆς τύχης κύριος ἦν, ἀλλ᾽ ἐκείνη τῶν πάντων, ibid. 321: τούτου γὰρ ἡ φύσις κυρία τοῦ δύνασθαι δὲ καὶ ἰσχύειν ἕτερα.

The expression κύριος γενόμενος (Plutarch, *Quaest. Conv.* VI, 8, 2 (II, 694c) often occurs in connexion with the military overpowering of a town. κύριος also connotes possession, e.g. of money, Demosthenes, *Or.* 21, 98; 27, 55 ff., etc., especially man's possession of control over himself: Plato, *Ep.* 7, 324b—εἰ θᾶττον ἐμαυτοῦ γενοίμην κύριος. So Aristotle, *Eth. Nic.* III 6, p. 1113b, 32—κύριος τοῦ μὴ μεθυσθῆναι, Plutarch, *Quaest. Conv.* VIII, 9, 2 (II, 731c)—αὐτοκρατὲς δὲ ἡ ψυχὴ καὶ κύριον, also *Apopth. Praef.* (II, 172d)—τῶν μὲν λόγων ἔφη κύριος αὐτὸς εἶναι, τῶν δὲ πράξεων τὴν τύχην. More generally it often means, " providing the decisive factor ": Plato, *Republic* IV, 429b—whether a city is brave or cowardly is decided by its soldiers, the others in the city οὐ . . . κύριοι ἂν εἶεν ἢ τοίαν αὐτὴν εἶναι ἢ τοίαν, " they have not got it in their hands ". Thus the δαίμων of a man in Dio Chrysostom, *Or.* 25, 1 is described as τὸ κρατοῦν ἑκαστοῦ, and the question whether it is something inside man or something ἔξωθεν ὂν ἄρχον τε καὶ κύριον τοῦ ἀνθρώπου is answered in the affirmative, and this then explains that kings, leaders and generals have been good or evil spirits (δαίμονες) for their subjects; thus to be κύριος means to exercise a powerful influence.

He who is *kurios* exercises a power which is not immediate, brutal or external, his power can take effect as unintelligibly and yet ineluctably as that of faith. It follows that *kurios* is also the right word to express " valid ", i.e. " having the force of law ". The transition may be seen in Andocides I, 87 ; ψήφισμα δὲ μηδὲν μήτε βουλῆς μήτε δήμου νόμου κυριώτερον εἶναι. In the case of laws which are operative, it means " of legal force ", " valid " : cf. Demosthenes, *Or.* 24, of the law, κύριος εἰ γενήσεται. So often in papyri of treaties, agreements, signatures, e.g. *Oxyr. Pap.* II, 261, 17 f. : κυρία ἡ συγγραφήι (a slip for συγγραφή)—A.D. 55. Of persons (with infinitive or participle), it means " plenipotentiary ", " entitled ", " commissioned " ; Demosthenes, *Or.* 59, 4, Eur, *Supplices* 1189 f. : οὗτος κύριος, τύραννος ὤν, πάσης ὑπὲρ γῆς Δαναϊδῶς ὁρκωμοτεῖν (to take an oath) ; with the participle, *Elephantine Papyri* I, 15 f. (a marriage settlement 311-310 B.C.)— κύριοι δὲ ἔστωσαν Ἡρακλείδης καὶ Δημητρία . . . τὰς συγγραφὰς αὐταὶ τὰς αὑτων φυλάσσοντες, Polybius, 6, 37, 8, κύριος δ' ἐστι καὶ ζημιῶν ὁ χιλίαρχος καὶ ἐνεχυράζων (to take a pledge) ; with the infinitive, Andoc. 4, 9 : τοὺς δικαστὰς ἀπολέσαι μὲν κυρίους εἶναι. With the genitive, it denotes " with full powers concerning ", Antiphon, *Or.* III, 1, 1 (ed. L. Gernet, 1923)— ὑπὸ . . . τῶν ψηφισαμένων, οἱ κύριοι πάσης τῆς πολιτείας εἰσίν, Isocrates, 19, 34— τὴν μητέρα καὶ τὴν ἀδελφὴν τῶν αὑτοῦ κυρίας . . . κατέστησε, Plato, *Laws*, XI, 929d—if the sick or demented father οἰκοφθορῇ . . . ὡς ὢν τῶν αὑτοῦ κύριος, the law empowers him to do what he will with his own. The *nomos* is *kurios basileus*, Plato, *Ep.* 8, 354c : the opposite is *turannos*. *Elephantine Papyri* 2, 4 f. (a will of 285-284 B.C.)—ἐὰν δέ τι πάσχῃ Καλλίστα Διονυσίου ζῶντος, κύριον εἶναι Διονύσιον τῶν ὑπαρχόντων. Hence *ta kuria* means "the legal power" in the state, Demosthenes, *Or.* 19, 259—τὰ κύρι' ἄττα ποτ' ἐστὶν ἐν ἑκάστῃ τῶν πόλεων.

kurios of the captured Andromache.[1] The only pre-Socratic reference to call for mention is Democritus' *mot*[2] τόλμα πρήξιος ἀρχή, τύχη δὲ τέλεος κυρίη—" is decisive with regard to the end ".

As a noun with a definite significance *kurios* first occurs in the first half of the fourth century B.C. and begins to be fixed in two meanings—the " lord " as the person with rights of disposing over a slave, Demosthenes, *Or.* 36, 28, 43 f.; 37, 51; 47, 14 f. (but *despotēs* is used some sixteen times of a master of slaves), Xenophon, *Oec.*, 9, 16, Aristotle, *Pol.* II, 9 (1269b, 9 f.) —lord of subject peoples, who τῶν ἴσων ἀξιοῦσιν ἑαυτοὺς τοῖς κυρίοις, lord of the house—Demosthenes, *Or.* 47, 60 (cf. n. 1 supra. In the sense of one who " is there for a purpose " who is put in charge of certain things and has them " under him ", probably also Antiphon, *Or.* II, 4, 7 (ed. L. Gernet, 1923)—of a slave who was not tortured—οὐδὲν θαυμαστὸν ἔπαθεν ὑπὸ τῶν κυρίων, cf. Plato, *Crito*, 44a—φασί γέ τοι δὴ οἱ τούτων κύριοι. The second meaning in which *kurios* begins to crystallise is the legal " spokesman " of a wife or a girl—Isaeus, 6, 32, Demosthenes, *Or.* 46, 15, etc. . . . . Both usages of the noun link on to the adjective in the sense of " plenipotentiary ". The idea of " legitimate " included in this is clear in the *Hibeh Papyri* (243-242 B.C.) 34, 3—a claim ἢ τὸ ὑποζύγιον ἀποδοῦναι τῷ κυρίῳ (the legal possessor), or to pay the price. How strong was the sense of legality in the word in Athens about 400 B.C. is shown in Aristophanes, *Plutus*, 6 f., where the lot of a slave is gloomily depicted : fate does not allow the legal *kurios*, namely the slave himself, to dispose of his

---

[1] *Kurios* is also the head of the family, *Oxyr. Pap.* II, 288, 36 (first century A.D.). But Plutarch calls the householder as such, *despotēs*, *Septem Sapientium Convivium*, 12 (II, 155d). This word occurs 106 times in Euripides, 17 in Aeschylus.

[2] Fr. 269 (II 115, 8 f., Diels).

body, but him who bought him—who has been called *despotēs* in line 2. . . . In Attic Greek *kurios* keeps the adjective's limitation to legal power of disposition (which it also never quite loses in Hellenistic Greek) : Dio Chrysostom in his speeches *De Servitute* (*Or.* 14 and 15) always uses *despotes* for the slave's lord. Typical of him and of Attic usage, is *Or.* 14, 22 : Odysseus as beggar οὐδὲν ἧττον βασιλεὺς ἦν καὶ τῆς οἰκίας κύριος. Lucian also uses *despotēs* as *kurios* is used in the *Koinē:* in *Dialogi Marini,* 7, 2, Zephyrus says of Io, ἡμῶν ἔσται δέσποινα, ὅντινα ἂν ἡμῶν ἐθέλῃ ἐκπέμψαι. Antiatticistes (*Anecd. Graec.* I, p. 102, 20) κύριαν οὔ φασι δεῖν λέγειν, ἀλλὰ κεκτημένην· τὸν δ κεκτημένον μὴ λέγεσθαι ἀντὶ τοῦ δεσπότου ... In the fragments of the Attic comic poets *despotēs* occurs fifty-six times, *despoina,* 11 ; where *kurios* occurs as a noun, that is mostly in contexts where *despotēs* does not fit or where the distinction between noun and adjective disappears ; cf. *Philemon* [1]—ἐμοῦ γάρ ἐστι κύριος μὲν εἷς ἀνήρ (the slave is speaking) τούτων δὲ καὶ σοῦ μυρίων τ' ἄλλων νόμος: here *kurios* means " has to speak "—*despotēs* would not express this so directly ; *Alexis,*[2] fr. 262 : if thou marriest, οὐδὲ σαυτοῦ κύριον ἔξεστιν εἶναι (cf. supra, p. 2, line 18) ; idem, fr. 149 : οὐχ ἀρχιτέκτων κύριος τῆς ἡδονῆς μόνος καθέστηκ'—enjoyment of art does not depend solely on the artist. *Kurios* means " the possessor " only in *Crito,*[3] μεγάλου κύριον βαλλαντίου . . . ποιήσας. In Menander, *kurios* occurs as a noun, meaning a child's spokesman (*Epitrepontes,* 89), a slave's lord (*Pericles,* 186), and in *Samia* 287 it is used of Ἔρως as ὁ τῆς ἐμῆς νῦν κύριος γνώμης. W. Schmid, in *Der Atticismus in seinen Hauptvertretern* (1887-1897) speaks of *kurios* only as an adjective in his

---

[1] *Comicorum, Atticorum Fragmenta* (ed. Kock) II, 486, fr. 31.

[2] Op. cit., II, 393.

[3] Op. cit., III, 354, fr. 3.

Register, Eustathius Thessalonicensis (*Opuscula*) has ὅπου γε ἡ εὐγενὴς ἀττικὴ γλῶσσα τὸν κύριον ἐπὶ ἀνδρὸς τίθησιν, ᾧ γυναῖκα ὁ νόμος συνέζευξε. Dionysius of Halicarnassus, *Antiquitates Romanae*, II, 27, 2, has τὴν ἐλευθερίαν εὑράμενος (sc. ὁ θεράπων) αὐτοῦ τὸ λοιπὸν ἤδη κύριός ἐστιν—which shows the same usage as is described above. The later relationship between *kurios* and *despotēs* is shown by Manuel Moschopulos (*c.* A.D. 1300) in his *Sylloge Vocum Atticarum*, s.v. *despotēs*: δεσπότης λέγεται πρὸς δοῦλον, κύριος δὲ πρὸς ἐλεύθερον, and s.v. *despoina*: δέσποινα λέγεται οὐ μόνον ἡ βασιλίς, ἀλλὰ καὶ ἡ τοῦ οἴκου δεσπότις, ἣν ἰδιωτικῶς κυρίαν φαμέν. Thus in Attic Greek *kurios* has a closely limited use. The broadening of the term seen in the N.T. belongs to the *Koinē*—especially the extended use of the noun.[1]

In the *Koinē despotēs* and *kurios* are widely used side by side. *Kurios* is the possessor of slaves and property. In the treaty between Miletus and Heraclea,[2] the legal proprietors of runaway slaves are called *kurioi*. But a distinction between the two words is still discernible. Epictetus uses both, often alternately, for the slave's master (e.g. *Diss*. IV, 1, 116). But he prefers *kurios* for the exposition of his concept of freedom, since this word is capable of a further application : in *Diss*. IV, 1, 59, πᾶς ὃς ἂν ἐξουσίαν ἔχῃ τῶν ὑπ᾽ αὐτοῦ τινος θελομένων πρὸς τὸ περιποιῆσαι ταῦτα ἢ ἀφελέσθαι is *kurios*, the rich are

---

[1] It must be specially stressed that Demosthenes does not *call* Philip *kurios*, but that *kurios* when used of him (always with a genitive) says that he is the one person given the full powers which Greek law gives to the people (*Or*. 18, 235 f., cf. 19, 64 ; 6, 6 ; 18, 201 ; 1, 4, etc. The noun which Demosthenes uses for the position of the king over his subjects is *despotēs* (*Or*. 5, 17 ; 6, 25 ; 15, 27 ; 18, 296 ; 19, 69 ; 20, 16). To be *kurios* means to have supreme sovereignty in one's hands, G. Busolt, *Griechische Staatskunde*, i. p. 304, and n. 4.

[2] Ditt. Syll³ 633, 95.

οἱ τὸν κύριον τὸν μέγαν ἔχοντες καὶ πρὸς τὸ ἐκείνου νεῦμα καὶ κίνημα ζῶντες, IV, 1, 145. The difference between the two words is clear from the changes in their use, *Diss.*, IV, 1, 12 f. : the senator asks who could compel him εἰ μὴ ὁ πάντων κύριος Καῖσαρ, to which Epictetus replies: οὐκοῦν ἕνα μὲν δεσπότην σαυτοῦ καὶ σὺ αὐτὸς ὡμολόγησας. The senator names the emperor *kurios*, as the one who has the power and right of disposing over everything, but from the point of view of Epictetus' concept of freedom he is thereby a slave who has his *despotēs* over him. Thus there easily enters into *despotēs* an element of hardness, as is also shown by Plutarch, *Lucullus*, 18 (I, 503a) a lady taken prisoner-of-war bewails her beauty as having secured her a *despotēs* instead of a husband. Of Philip, the father of Alexander, it was reported that he said μᾶλλον πολὺν χρόνον ἐθέλειν χρηστὸς ἢ δεσπότης ὀλίγον καλεῖσθαι (Plutarch, *Apophthegamata*, *Philippus*, 4 (II, 177d). . . . But *kurios* is he who has *exousia*. The element of legality which is also inherent in this word, is occasionally more clearly apparent : Plutarch, *Aratus*, 9 (I, 1031b), says of those who have been exiled : κατελθόντες δὲ οἱ πλεῖστοι πένητες ὧν κύριοι πρότερον ἦσαν ἐπελαμβάνοντο. Again, κύριοι τῆς ὁλκάδος are those who give the word on board ship (Plutarch, *De Mario* 37 (I, 427a) ; Aratus says to Philip of Macedon, *Aratus* 50 (I, 1050e) : " If you approach them with trust and friendliness τῶν μὲν (of the Cretans) ἡγεμών, τῶν δὲ (the Peloponnesians) κύριος ἤδη καθέστηκας." The explanation of both terms is given shortly beforehand. " Although you Philip, have not won any fixed position, πάντες ἑκουσίως σοι ποιοῦσι τὸ προστασσόμενον " ; *Kurios* is he whose authority wins obedience. Cf. Plutarch, *Apophthegamata Laconica*, *Pausanias Plistonactis*, 1 (II, 230 f.) : τοὺς νόμους . . . τῶν ἀνδρῶν, οὐ τοὺς ἄνδρας τῶν νόμων κυρίους εἶναι δεῖ. *Kurios* denotes the lord of a slave in

Plutarch, *Apophthegmata*, *Agathocles*, 2 (II, 176e). Finally, the gods are called *Kurioi* as those who dispose over some sphere of life : *An recte dictum sit latenter esse vivendum* 6 (II, 1130a)—τὸν δὲ τῆς ἐναντίας (set over against the sun) κύριον μοίρας . . . Ἅιδην ὀνομάζουσιν, *Def. Orac.* 29 (II, 426a—cf. *supra*, p. 1, *ad fin.*), *Quaest. Conv.* V, 3, 1, 4 (II, 675 f.)—Poseidon and Dionysius τῆς ὑγρᾶς καὶ γονίμου κύριοι δοκοῦσιν ἀρχῆς εἶναι. *Kurios* is the word which the inferior is glad to use of the superior, since it emphasises the authority and legality of his position. Thus Cassius was greeted in Rhodes as βασιλεὺς καὶ κύριος, and the answer cuts like a knife : οὔτε βασιλεὺς οὔτε κύριος, τοῦ δὲ κυρίου καὶ βασιλέως φονεὺς καὶ κολαστής (Plutarch, *Brutus* 30 (I, 998b), while Brutus himself says (op. cit. 22—I, 994c) : οἱ δὲ πρόγονοι . . . ἡμῶν οὐδὲ πράους δεσπότας ὑπέμεινον.

Kurios is he who can dispose of things or persons, *despotēs* he who possesses a thing or person. That shows how far the two words touch one another, and how far they are separate. The more popular the speech and the nearer to the time of the N.T. the more does *kurios* oust *despotēs* ; the closer the contact with the written word and the nearer the beginning of the Hellenistic era, the greater is the authoritative and legal element in *kurios*. We may end with the interesting passage from Lucan, *Nigrinus*, 26 : the philosopher despises earthly goods, as he maintains ὅτι τούτων μὲν φύσει οὐδενός ἐσμεν κύριοι, νόμῳ δὲ καὶ διαδοχῇ τὴν χρῆσιν αὐτῶν εἰς ἀόριστον παραλαμβάνοντες ὀλιγοχρόνιοι δεσπόται νομιζόμεθα. *Kurios* and *despotēs* cannot be confused here.

Not everyone who can dispose over a thing or person is therefore called *kurios* without qualification. In general the (legal) owner (also of slaves) receives the title *kurios*. But gradually the usage established itself of addressing members of a higher class as *kurie* (or *kuria*) and speaking about them as *ho kurios*, in the case of officials often adding the title of the office. The letters of the general Apollonius of the beginning of the second century A.D. show that not only his employees and slaves but, e.g. the villagers address him as *kurie*, *Giessen Papyri*, 61, 17 (A.D. 119), whereas a wealthy ναύκληρος calls him alternately φίλτατε and κύριε. (*Giessen Papyri*, 11, 12, and 20—A.D. 118) and his family (with one exception, *vide infra*) does not so address him. Appollonius for his part addresses his superiors as ἡγεμὼν κύριε (*Giessen Papyri*, 41, I, 4, 9, and 13). This usage can be traced back to the first century A.D. : Epictetus has high officials (*Diss.* IV, 1, 57), philosophers being feted (III, 23, 11 and 19) the doctor (II, 15, 15, and III, 10, 15) and the μάντις (II, 7, 9) addressed as *kurie*, the cynic even as κύριε ἄγγελε καὶ κατάσκοπε (III, 22, 38) : in his *Encheiridion*, 40, he says generally that wives of fourteen years standing were addressed as *kuriai* by their husbands. According to Dio Chrysostom LXI, 20, 1, Nero as lute-player addressed the spectators as *kurioi mou*, while *kurios hēgemōn* occurs as early as A.D. 45 in *Oxyr. Pap.* II, 283, 18 : similarly in *Oxyr. Pap.* I, 37, II, 8 (A.D. 49) τὰ ὑπὸ τοῦ κυρίου ἡγεμόνος κριθέντα, and in the year A.D. 71-72 (*Tebtunis Papyri* 302, 11 and 20) we find attached to *hēgemōn* the phrase σοῦ τε τοῦ κυρίου γράψαντος. An apparently unique example dates back to the first century B.C.—τῷ κυρίῳ στρατηγῷ—*Aegyptische Urkunden zu Berlin*, 1819, 2 (60-59 B.C.). When, as early as the first century A.D. (op. cit. 665, II, 18) a son addresses his father as *kurie mou*, when that is probably used by Hermaios to his brother, the general Apollonius (*Giessen Papyri* 85, 16—early second century A.D.), that may still be the expression of a certain subordination : but finally even a father addresses his son as *kurie*, *Oxyr. Pap.* I, 123, 1—κυρίῳ μου υἱῷ Διονυσοθέωνι ὁ πατὴρ χαίρειν ; and line 24—κύριε υἱέ (third and fourth century A.D.). See further F. J. Dölger, *Antike und Christentum* V (1936), pp. 211-17.

Even before the beginning of the Constantine epoch, *despotēs* begins to oust *kurios* in every sphere. In *Oxyr. Pap.* I, 67, 10 (A.D. 338) *despotia* is used to designate legal ownership, but the address *despota hēgemōn* is used as early as A.D. 266 (*Tebtunis Papyri*, 326, 3) and in the letter from a father to his son mentioned above (*Oxyr. Pap.* I, 123) the former calls the addressee in line 7 *despota mou* and speaks of *despoina mou mētēr humōn* (l. 22). In the emperor's titles, too, *kurios* was more and more replaced by *despotēs*.

The whole development can thus be summarised by saying that *kurios*, originally the plenipotentiary, the person entitled to dispose, discarded the element of arbitrariness which was easily associated with *despotēs*, and for that very reason was used in the first instance by slaves to their masters in a kind of delicate flattery [1] and so gradually ousted *despotēs* in everyday speech. For the same reasons, however, since *despotēs* more strongly stressed the immediacy and unlimitedness of possession, the latter term was once again preferred in the age of dawning Byzantinism.

Thus at the beginning of the Hellenistic era, *kurios* was still relatively seldom used as a noun and in the relatively limited sense of legal lord and possessor and of plenipotentiary. The later practice of calling gods and rulers *kurios* must have developed in the Hellenistic epoch. There is no proof that Philip of Macedon or Alexander the Great or any of the first of the Diadochoi were called *kurioi* any more than that any gods were in this period. For the well-known passage in the paean

---

[1] In two letters, recorded in Josephus, *Ant.* XVII, 137 and 139, the slave calls her mistress her *kuria*, whereas Josephus (loc. cit. § 138) calls her *despoina*.

which the Athenians sang in honour of Demetrius
Poliorketes [1]—πρῶτον μὲν εἰρήνην ποιήσον, φίλτατε, κύριος
γὰρ εἰ σύ—is to be translated " for thou canst do it,
thou hast it in thy hand " (vide supra, p. 2, ad init.).
The earliest instance of kurios being used of a god is in
the LXX, which has already been shown [2] to be most
unlikely to be linking on to some already established
usage. The earliest instance of the developing Hellenistic usage is the treaty between Philip VI of
Macedonia and Hannibal reported by Polybius
(VII, 9 5) : ἐφ' ὧτ' εἶναι σῳζομένους . . . κυρίους
καρχηδονίους καὶ Ἀννίβαν τὸν στρατηγόν. Next follows the
Greek translation of the Egyptian Pharoah-title in the
form kurios basileiōn [3] and kurios triakontaetēridōn.[4]

[1] Athenaeus, VI, 63 (p. 253e). See Foerster, op. cit. p. 110.
But the passage is differently interpreted : see Baudissin, op.
cit. II, p. 288 : but to interpret it as an adjective (as does W.
Schubert, Die Religiöse Haltung des frühen Hellenismus (1937), p. 19)
seems to me to fit the context.

[2] An argumentum e silentio from the silence of the sources is not
entirely convincing (though vide infra, p. 19, ad init.), but it
gains weight in the context of the philological evidence.

[3] Deissmann, Licht vom Osten, p. 300, n. 2 (Ptolemy Philopator,
221-205 B.C.), C.I.G., 4697 (196 B.C.).

[4] Ditt. Or. 90, line 2. With these two notes cf. Baudissin, op.
cit. II, p. 288, nn. 2 and 3.

II. GODS AND RULERS AS *KURIOI*

An indispensable constituent of every religion is the element of legitimate power, i.e. the power in which man must acknowledge authority and bow before its superiority. If this element of legitimacy is lacking, *religio* is replaced by the fear of spirits against which man tries to defend himself in every way, against which he fights. If the element of power is absent, then the divinity is only an idea. The two together, power and right, as an unified conception, are bound up with the personality of their bearer. For right and its counterpart, responsibility, are categories only to be used between persons. In Greek religion, too, the conception of God does not altogether lack the element of personal, legitimate power. Its expression is the term " Lord ". Now *despotēs* (*despoina*) is applied to the Gods in classical Greek and occasionally also later, and denotes the relationship of the Gods to nature and to men. But the dividing line between Greeks and " Barbarians " in the whole human sphere, political as well as religious, is precisely that the Greeks are fundamentally averse from regarding their gods as lords and themselves as slaves (*douloi*). This is bound up with the fact that in Greek religion the basic personal act, the creativity of God, is almost entirely lacking.

(1) Κύριος *for gods and rulers in classical Greek*

The word *kurios*, it is true, was also applied to the Greek gods from the classical era up to the imperial epoch, first as adjective then more as substantive, and applied when the intention was to predicate that they can dispose over distinctive spheres of life.

13

Pindar, *Isthm.* V, 53 has Ζευς ὁ πάντων κύριος ; Plato, *Laws*, XII, 13 (966c) says the φύλακες must know of the gods ὡς εἰσίν τε καὶ ὅσης φαίνονται κύριοι δυνάμεως, (cf. *Republic*, VII, 517c) ;[1] Xenophon, *Memorabilia*, I, 4, 9, says that against the proof of God from the *nous* of man the objection is raised : " οὐ γὰρ ὁρῶ τοὺς κυρίους ". In his *Oeconomicus* VI, 1, he says that " with the gods one must begin ὡς τῶν θεῶν κυρίων ὄντων οὐδὲν ἧττον τῶν εἰρηνικῶν ἢ τῶν πολεμικῶν ἔργων. Demosthenes, *Or.* 60, 21, has ὁ πάντων κύριος δαίμων. In his *Ep.* 4, 6, he says of the gods : ἁπάντων τῶν ἀγαθῶν ἐγκρατεῖς ὄντας κυρίους εἶναι καὶ αὐτοὺς ἔχειν καὶ δοῦναι τοῖς ἄλλοις. Sosiphanes, fr. 3, has

> ἤν δ᾿ εὐτυχῆτε, μηδὲν ὄντες εὐθέως
> ἴσ᾿ οὐρανῷ φρονεῖτε, τὸν δὲ κύριον
> Ἅιδην παρεστῶτ᾿ οὐχ ὁρᾶτε πλησίον.

Dio Chrysostom (*Or.* 37, 11) calls Poseidon and Helios *kurios* respectively of water and fire ; Plutarch (*Isis and Osiris*, 35—II, 365a) says that the Greeks consider Dionysus *kurios kai archēgos* not only of wine, but also πάσης ὑγρᾶς φύσεως ; also that Poseidon and Dionysus τῆς ὑγρᾶς καὶ γονίμου κύριοι δοκοῦσιν ἀρχῆς εἶναι (*Quaest. Conviv.* V, 3, 1). Aelius Aristides (*Or.* 37, 17) says that *Nikē* (victory) is not *kuria* of Athene, but Athene is *kuria* of *Nikē*. In Plutarch, *Isis and Osiris*, 40 (II, 367a), Isis is called ἡ κυρία τῆς γῆς θεός, Osiris is greeted as ἁπάντων κύριος (ibid. 12—II, 355e) and as ὁ τῶν ἀρίστων πάντων ἡγεμὼν καὶ κύριος (ibid. 49—II, 371a). Philo of Byblos says of Beelsamen ὁ ἐστι παρὰ Φοίνιξι κύριος οὐρανοῦ, Ζεὺς δὲ παρ᾿ Ἕλλησι. In similar

---

[1] Plato, *Ep.* 6, 323d has : τὸν τῶν πάντων θεὸν ἡγεμόνα τῶν τε ὄντων καὶ τῶν μελλόντων, τοῦ τε ἡγεμόνος καὶ αἰτίου πατέρα κύριον ἐπομνύντας. Here θεὸς ἡγεμών corresponds to πατὴρ κύριος. Possibly *kurios* stresses the position of the " Father " as head of the family. Cf. n. 1, p. 5.

strain Epictetus (*Diss.* IV, 1, 12) speaks of ὁ πάντων κύριος Καῖσαρ (*vide infra*, p. 27, *ad fin.* and p. 24, note 2).

It is to be observed, however, that in contrast to the oriental and Egyptian divine names, the gods are not actually here named as *kurios* of their own sphere, and that thus the being lord is not their vital characteristic, whereas in Babylon and Egypt they are named precisely in virtue of what they are lords of : " May the deeds of Marduk, the lord of the Gods, be seen by all the gods and goddesses, Anu, Enlil, the lord of the ocean, the sovereign Ea." [1] This situation is connected with the fundamental structure of Greek theology, namely that for the Greeks the gods are in principle only the " basic forms of reality ", and so do not personally confront the world and mankind as creators or designers and are also not lords of the reality which holds together all realities, namely fate. The latter is rather, and often, an independent entity alongside the gods. Since gods and men " breath from one mother " and are organically connected limbs of one reality, their mutual relationship cannot be described by *kurios-doulos* terminology.[2] Man has no basic personal responsibility to these gods, nor do they confront mankind with punishment. A prayer to them is

[1] A. Ungnad, *Die Religion der Babylonier und Assyrer* (1921), p. 174, etc. In Egypt the gods become not only " lords " of a town (e.g. G. Roeder, *Urkunden zur Religion des alten Aegyptien*, p. 5, on Amon-Re as lord of Karnak) but also lord of eternity, of existence (Roeder, op. cit. p. 5) lord of justice, lord of corn, (loc. cit. p. 7), Aton is also called lord of heaven, lord of earth, (p. 69). A transferred use of " lord " is also found frequently (as with *ba'al* in the O.T.), e.g. lord of worship (p. 5, *ad fin.*). Further information in A. Erman and H. Grapow, *Wörterbuch der ägyptischen Sprache*, vol. ii (1928), s.v. *nb*.

[2] Conceivably the reason why *despotēs* (*despoina*) could be applied in the classical era to gods is because it suggests the " paterfamilias ", i.e. the organic link between the human and divine?

fundamentally illogical—as is the fact that Zeus turns up again as lord of fate. But that only shows that a further *motif* is appearing—that a theology in which the gods are only the basic forms of reality is bound to disintegrate.

Each passing conception of the lordship of the gods is indissolubly connected with the contemporary ideas of lordship-relations in the whole of life. If the gods are the epitome of reality, it is a question of finding this epitome of reality in other spheres. The political consequence of this is democracy, in which each individual contributes towards comprehending the depths of reality. In so far as the Greek " serves " the laws, he freely submits to what binds him, which he has himself, by his powers of reason, recognised as such, and to the formation and ratification of which he has himself contributed. Yet Law is not simply what the citizens resolve, but stands above them : that is shown by the passage of Andocides quoted on page 3, line 6.

However distant the Hellenistic monarchies may appear to be from Greek democracy, however much the Greeks later repeatedly hailed the proclamation of their " freedom ", it must nevertheless be stressed that the Hellenistic worship of the ruler had roots in the classical Greek spirit. For in the ruler was crystallised, to a special degree, the divine, of which the world is full ; he did not need the ratification of the people, since the latter's decisions would of course agree with those of the ruler who shares in " virtue " to an unparalleled degree. He is *theos*, *theos epiphanēs*, *neos Dionysos*, etc., but not *kurios*, he is not contrasted with the people, he is only inspired to a special degree by the divine which lives in all Greeks. The Hellenistic ruler is *nomos empsuchos*.[1]

[1] E. R. Goodenough, *The Political Philosophy of Hellenistic Kingship*, in Yale Classical Studies, i (1928), pp. 55-102.

(2) *Gods and rulers as lords in the Orient and in Egypt*

For orientals the gods are lords of reality, they have fate in their hands. To the gods who have created him the individual man owes personal responsibility, just as they intervene in his life with punishments.[1] From these two standpoints it is essential that the gods should there be called " lords ", lords over the world and its components, lords over fate, lords over men. There is nothing here of what is essential among the Greeks—that reality shows itself to men to be divine, and that man as a free agent takes up an attitude towards it. As the gods ordain what is right, so the ruler proclaims it to the subjects, and these have no other course open to them but to subject themselves to it in silence. This is what the Greeks felt to be servile. But in the East there was a strong feeling that the operation of justice demanded a personal authorisation. That leads to the oriental worship of the ruler. There the king is not conceived as a new manifestation of the divine, but the power which he has and the justice which he administers sets him above the level of mankind, and near to that of the gods to whom he owes his position. As king, as dispenser of justice, the ruler stands above men and can therefore, since the administration of justice has been handed over to him by the gods, give unconditional orders to men, who must obey him as unconditionally as they obey the gods. Everything here depends upon the personal contrast between God and man.

(3) *The Hellenistic Κύριος*

The consideration of the use of the Hellenistic title of *kurios* for gods and rulers demands a bird's-eye view of the evidence.

[1] Cf. The Babylonian penitential psalms, e.g. Ungnad, op. cit. p. 220. " I suffer as though I did not fear my God, or my goddess. Sorrow, sickness, destruction and decay are fallen to my lot ! "

(a) *The dates of its use*. No instance of *kurios* applied
to gods or rulers (except for *kurios* with the genitive,
supra, p. 3, *ad fin*. and p. 7, note 1) is earlier than
the first century B.C.[1] The earliest instance is *kurios*
used of Isis, in Egypt : C.I.G. 4897a (99-90 B.C.) ;
Cf. C.I.G. 4898, 4899, 4904, 4917, 4930b, 4931, Ditt.
Or. 186, 8 f., all first century B.C. As early as 81 B.C.
we find the formula προσκυνήσας τὴν κυρίαν θεὰν "Ισιν
(C.I.G. 4936d addenda)—all from Philae. Similarly
it is used of the god Soknopaios (Seknebtynis) in the
first century B.C. : ὡς θέλει ὁ Σεκνεβτῦνις ὁ κύριος θεός
(*Tebtunis Papyri*, 284, 5 f.). From Gizeh comes the
dedication of a building τῷ θεῷ καὶ κυρίῳ Σοκνοπαίῳ
(Ditt. Or. 655, 24 B.C.). In the time of Augustus or
Tiberius we have the Syrian inscription with the
formula θεὸς κρόνος κύριος (Ditt. Or. 606).

Of rulers, *kurios basileus* is found often in Egypt
between 64 and 50 B.C. (B.G.U. 1767, 1 ; 1768, 9 ;
1816, 3 ; Ditt. Or. 186, 8) : in 52 B.C. there is mention of
festivals τοῖς κυρίοις θεοῖς μεγίστοις—referring to Ptolemy
XIII and his co-rulers (*Berlin Akad.* (1902) 1096 :
similarly C.I.G. 4717, l.25 and 29). . . . Similarly
Augustus is named θεὸς καὶ κύριος Καῖσαρ
Αὐτοκράτωρ 12 B.C. in Egypt (B.G.U. 1197, I, 15—in
part restored) ; cf. B.G.U. 1200, 10 ff., and *Oxyr. Pap.*
VIII, 1143, 4 : θυσίας καὶ σπονδὰς ὑπὲρ τοῦ θεοῦ καὶ
κυρίου Αὐτοκράτορος (first century A.D.) ; Herod the
Great was called βασιλεὺς Ἡρώδης κύριος (Ditt. Or.
415) ; similarly Agrippa I and II (ibid. 418, 423, 425,
426) : in Upper Egypt Queen Candace was called, in

[1] J. J. E. Hondius, *Supplementum Epigraphicum Graecum*, iii
(1929), nos, 510-11, says that two Thracian inscriptions, one with
(κυρ)ίῳ Διί, the other with (κυ)ρίῳ Ἀσκληπιῷ, date from the
third century B.C. But the *Revue des études anciennes* XXVI
(1924), 32, and notes 1 and 2, shows that this is an error or mis-
print—they are from the third century A.D.

13 B.C., ἡ κυρία βασίλισσα (Mitteis-Wilcken, I, 2, 4). A ptolemaic general is called, in 51 B.C., ὁ θεότατος καὶ κύριος στρατηγός (B.G.U. 1838, 1—cf. 1819, 2).

Thus in Egypt *kurios* occurs within a life-span, used of gods, rulers and high officials. Since we have a considerable number of Greek documents of every kind from the preceding centuries in Egypt, in which *kurios* does not occur in this usage, it is not to be supposed that gaps in our material give us an essentially false picture of the time when *kurios* first appears in these connections, nor that new discoveries will make any essential difference to this picture.

In Syria, although the situation could conceivably be different, since we have no sacred Greek inscriptions from there from the second and third centuries B.C. (Baudissin, op. cit. II, 258), it may well be the case that there, too, the Greek *kurios* was not applied to gods and rulers before the first century B.C. The oldest Syrian evidence for *kurios* in the sense discussed is the inscription already mentioned (Ditt. Or. 606) in which besides Kronos, the imperial house is also named: ὑπὲρ τῆς τῶν κυρίων Σεβαστῶν σωτηρίας, lines 1 and 2. This situation is to be explained from the fact that it was not till the first century before Christ that the counter-stream from the East began, which poured the oriental ideas of lordship into Greek moulds.

It is noticeable that *kurios* almost immediately occurs in close connexion with the substantives *theos*, *basileus*, *stratēgos* (without any intervening *kai*). This usage cannot possibly mark the beginning, but it denotes an end. But since it is no ending of any Greek development, then it must be a translation of a long-existing Egyptian and Syrian usage. There the word corresponding to *kurios* was tacked on to terms such as god or king, without any conjunction (*vide infra*, p. 1052, 31).

3

(b) *The area of its use.* So far as concerns the geo-
graphical dissemination of the use of *kurios* for gods,
we do best to begin with Egypt. It is used predica-
tively once each of Ammon, Anubis, Apoll, Asclepius,
the Dioscuri, Horogebthios, Priotos, Rhodosternos,
Sruptichis, twice of Soknopaeus, three times of Pan,
four times of Bes, nine of Mandulis, sixteen of Hermes,
thirty-eight times each of Sarapis and Isis.[1] Outside
Egypt we find Egyptian gods called *kurios*, e.g. Sarapis
in Asia Minor, Crete and Italy, Helios in Spain, Isis
in Asia Minor and Rome. Moreover, according to
Oxyr. Pap. XI, 1380, κυρεία is the official name for Isis
in Heraclia Pelagos (ll. 61-2), and she was also addressed
as κυρία ῏Ισι (l. 142) and often called *kuria* with the
genitive of the sphere ruled over ; so with Horus and
Hermes (ll. 210-11 and 265-6). Plutarch speaks
similarly of Osiris (1046, 20 ff.) and in a hymn to Isis,
from Cyrene,[2] Isis is four times called *kuria* with a
noun in the genitive. Of the 119 times I have counted
kurios in Egypt, in ninety-five it occurs in the phrase
τὸ προσκύνημά τινος ποιεῖν παρὰ τῷ κυρίῳ (τῇ κυρίᾳ)
with the name of the god following, or similar phrases
connected with a προσκύνημα.

In Syria it occurs of various gods, especially Athene
and Zeus, less often in Arabia ; once each of Athene
(Allat) and Helios—certainly Syrian gods—in Spain.

In Asia Minor *kurios* occurs once each of Asclepius,
Hermes, Sarapis, Tiamos, Zeus, twice each of Helios,
Isis, Sabazios and Apoll, thrice of Nemesis, four times
of Πατρίς, thirteen of Artemis. The Ephesian

---

[1] The figures given here and below make no claim to complete-
ness : but the material from which they are drawn is so comprehensive that the conclusions drawn from them are most
unlikely to be disproved. They are drawn from Drexler's list in
Roscher's Lexicon, supplemented by the Papyri.

[2] W. Peek, *Der Isishymnus von Andros und verwandte Texte* (1930)
pp. 122 ff.

Artemis is once called *kuria* in Italy, and is probably referred to in two further inscriptions in Italy which speak of κυρία Ἄρτεμις (without Ἐφεσία).

Besides these, *kurios* (*kuria*) occurs without names of gods four times in Syria, and once there in the phrase θεῷ οὐρανίῳ πατρώῳ τῷ κυρίῳ ; [1] and often in the phrase ὁ κύριος θεός in Egypt.

On the other hand it is to be observed that Jupiter Heliopolitanus is only called *kurios* once, and Jupiter Dolichenus, never.

The result of all this is that *kurios* as a divine predicate was common only where it corresponded to some native, non-Greek usage and scarcely at all moved away from these regions. When used of gods, it is fundamentally a translation of foreign usage and no more. To corresponding with the very common use of 'ādhôn in Semitic inscriptions, the number of cases to be expected of κύριος in Syrian Greek inscriptions should be considerably larger. The Greek κύριος is relatively less frequently used in Syria than its Semitic equivalent, thus the writers of Greek inscriptions in Syria have often shunned it.[2]

---

[1] *Kurios* is also used of various gods in Thrace, but only once on the Greek mainland of πατρίς, in Sparta. For the Gnostic examples see Baudissin, op. cit. ii, p. 270, n. 2 : they are not here cited, nor are the Magical texts, which contain much that is old but many very different influences as well. Κύριος in astrological texts, despite E. Peterson's contention in *Byzantinisch-Neugriechirche Jahrbücher*, V (1926-7), p. 224, does not help us, as becomes clear from the course of the enquiry.

[2] As a random test, in the section of P. le Bas' and W. H. Waddington's great work *Inscriptions Grecques et latines recueilliés en Grèce et en Asie Mineure*, III (1870) concerned with Syrian inscriptions (nos. 1826-2677) Zeus is called *kurios* 6 times, but 5 times only Zeus, once θέος Ζεύς, once Ζεὺς κεραύνιος, once Ζεὺς ὕψιστος, 5 times Ζεὺς ὕψιστος καὶ ἐπήκοος, 5 times he has various other predicates. . . . Altogether 20 κύριος-passages stand over against 106 other names for a god.

(c) *Its meaning when used of gods.* It follows that the significance and content of *kurios* applied to gods, must be extracted in essentials from indigenous linguistic usage. But the Greek evidence also clearly shows a definite trend.

First, the predicate *kurios* is not intended to distinguish great or dominating gods from lesser, subordinate divinites.[1] In Syria there is no place for any such distinction, and in Egypt local divinites of small importance are also called *kurios*.[2] Nor is it a circle of divinites specially worshipped that are so named. Our observations point rather to the conclusion that *kurios* gives expression to the personal relationship of an individual to a god. For Egypt the noticeable frequency of *kurios* in *proskunēmata*, which represent a prayer or petition, may be mentioned first. Next, *kurios* is especially common in inscriptions conveying thanks : in the case of the Ephesian Artemis *kuria* only occurs in connexion with the phrase εὐχαριστῶ σοι, κυρία Ἄρτεμι,[3] and the same is true of Egyptian gods . . . Sarapis[4] and Mandulis (C.I.G. 5070), Hermes[5] and Nemesis,[6] and, slightly differently, the Dioscuri.[7] In petitionary prayer Sarapis is addressed as *kurie*[8] and the same address is found in consultations of the oracle[9] and the invocation to Helios to exact vengeance.[10] A personal relationship to an

[1] Baudissin, op. cit. ii, pp. 271 ff.

[2] Cf. the list given above (p. 20).

[3] *British Museum Greek Inscriptions*, 578c, 580, 582a, 586a, 587b, 588, 588b, 590 ; Hondius, op. cit. iv (1930), 535, 9 f.

[4] B.G.U. 423, 6 ff. (second century A.D.).

[5] *Giessen Papyri* 85, 6 f.

[6] Hondius, op. cit. vii (1934), 804.

[7] . . . Drexler (in Roscher), 1760.

[8] . . . Ibid. 1763, and C.I.G. 4710 (Lycopolis) . . . and 4712b.

[9] *Oxyr. Pap.* VIII, 1148, 1 (first century A.D.) . . .

[10] J.H.S. v (1884), p. 253, no. 4 ; Hondius, op. cit. vi (1932), 803.

unnamed god appears in the inscription καθαρμοῖς κὲ
θυσίαις ἐ[τίμησα τὸν κ]ύριον ἵνα μυ(=μοι) το ἐμὸν σῶ[μα
σῴζ]ει (= σῴζοι),[1] and presumably also in that well-
known invitation to the κλείνη τοῦ κυρίου Σαράπιδος [2] as in
the ἐγκατοχήσας τῷ κυρίῳ Σαράπιδι.[3] In Syria *kurios*
occurs as a name for god very often in the dedication
of consecrated memorials, in which the author of the
monument expresses his personal relationship to this
god. On the other hand, in contexts in which a
personal relation to the divinity is not expressly implied, *kurios* is used but seldom.[4] There remains
(besides texts of which the context is not clear) a
group of inscriptions containing *kurios*, in which the
author designates himself as standing under the
command of the divinity he calls *kurios*: Λούκιος . . .
πεμφθεὶς ὑπὸ τῆς κυρίας Ἀταργάτης ; [5] κατ᾽ἐπιταγὴν
τῆς κυρίας Ἀρτέμιδος ; [6] cf. *Tebtunis Papyri*, 284, 2 ff.
(first century B.C.).

Thus *kurios* is especially used as the expression of a
personal relationship of men to god, expressing itself
in prayer, thanksgiving and devotion, and as correlative to *doulos*, whereby the person concerned addresses
the god whom he calls *kurios* as his master. But we
must now distinguish this range of thought from the
power of gods over nature, or parts thereof. It can be
no mere chance that in the case of Isis and Sarapis, the
two who are most often called *kurios* (*kuria*), the idea of

[1] *J.H.S.* viii (1887), p. 388, no. 17.
[2] *Oxyr. Pap.* I, 110, III, 523, XII, 1484, XIV, 1755 (first to
third centuries A.D.).
[3] C.I.G. 3163 (Smyrna).
[4] Examples of this are in Le Bas-Waddington, op. cit.
1879. . . . Hondius, op. cit. ii (1925), 830, 3 ff. . . . and 832.
I have found thirteen such texts where a personal relationship of
the speaker to the god named *Kurios* is not discernible.
[5] Le Bas-Waddington, 1890.
[6] Hondius, op. cit. iii (1929), 691 (Mytilene).

dominion over nature and fate most clearly confronts
us. For Isis the best sources are *Oxyr. Pap.* XI, 1380,
121 ff., the Hymn of Cyrene (p. 20, n. 2 *supra*) and
Apuleius, *Metamorphoses* XI, 5 ; for Sarapis, the
Sarapis-Aretologies.[1] The *motif* of power in *kurios*
reaches its zenith in the Hermetic writings.[2]

Thus the Greek evidence leads to a result similar to
the analysis of the meaning of the corresponding
Semitic word arrived at by Baudissin in his detailed
discussion. *Kurios* corresponds not to the Semitic *ba'al*,
but to the Phoenicean Canaanite '*ādhôn*, Fem. *rabbath*
and Aramaic *mârê'*. These words were frequently
tacked on as epithets before a god's name, as was also
the Hellenistic *kurios*, and they were generally linked
with a personal suffix, relating to the worshipper of
the god, and occasionally also added as the genitive
of a personal pronoun to the Greek *kurios* as a divine
name.[3] The personal relationship expressed in this
personal suffix or personal pronoun is not found among
the Greeks and Romans.[4] This is connected with the

---

[1] O. Weinreich, *Neue Urkunden zur Sarapis-Religion* (1919).

[2] The content of *Kurios* in the *Corpus Hermeticum* (I, 6, V, 2,
XIII, 17, 21) is not so clear as in the rest of the Hermetic literature, in which it is linked with expressions of universality : ὁ τῶν ὅλων κύριος, Κόρη Κόσμου, 25 ; πάντων
κύριος, fr. 12, 23, 24, 29, 33 : Lord and creator of all :
Ascl. I, 8 : fr. 32 ; . . . Ascl. III, 29b : " summa vero
gubernationis summo illi domino paret ", Ascl. III, 19c ; especially Ascl. III, 20a—" deus etenim vel pater vel dominus omnium
quocumque [alio] nomine . . . nuncupatur. . . . Non enim
spero totius maiestatis effectorem omniumque rerum patrem
vel dominum uno posse quamvis e multis conposito nuncupari
nomine ". " Deus " and " Pater " are also linked in Ascl. III,
22b, 23b, 26a . . . (Quotations from *Corp. Herm.* ed. W. Scott,
1924.)

[3] ἐκ τῶν τοῦ κυρίου αὐτῶν θεοῦ Ἀμέρου, Hondius, op.
cit. vii (1934), 1069, 7 (Arabia). . . . *Louvre Papyri*, 19, 5.

[4] Baudissin, op. cit. iii, p. 556 and n. 1.

general difference between Oriental and Greek religion discussed above. That the correlative to this concept of lord is " slave ", in Greek *doulos*, is shown by some inscriptions (*vide supra*, p. 23, lines 11 ff.) and, for the Semitic sphere, by the frequent use of *'ebhedh* in personal names linked with a god. Now it is not possible to see, in the use of " lord " linked with the god's name, only the *motif* of personal belonging to, and not also the *motif* of personal authority which the worshipper ascribes to his god, and which on his side expresses subjection of the will. Nor is it possible to separate the element of power from that of greatness, as Baudissin once contended.[1] If all Semitic personal names linked with a god which are based upon some other word than " slave " express something of what the god has done, or will do, for the salvation of his worshippers, or else name some characteristic on which is based the certainty or the hope of intervention of the god on behalf of his worshipper,[2] then it is implied that the god has the power to act thus on behalf of his slave. Whether his sphere of power perhaps extends only to what is dependent upon the development of the cor- poration, or of individual members of it,[3] is here immaterial, though it is also important for N.T. times that the power of the god was always extending and in Palmyra the divine names *mârē' 'âlmā'* and *mâre' khol* are found.[4] And if for orientals too the power of the ruler in earliest times expressed itself not in ruling but in judging,[5] the administration of justice pre- supposes an authority which will be obeyed, i.e. in

---

[1] Op. cit. p. 631. " The designation of the god as lord ex- presses man's bowing before a greatness which only permits of humble adoration rather than a power before which he stands helpless."

[2] Op. cit. p. 527. [3] Op. cit. p. 625.

[4] Op. cit. pp. 684 f. [5] Op. cit. pp. 613 ff.

fact some " power ". . . .[1] But the linking of a personal suffix with the designation " lord " also indicates that " even in primitive conditions, his (the slave's) relationship to his lord as his property provides also the guarantee of protection against dangers from other people ".[2]

In Hebrew *ba'al* denotes more the owner, *'ādhôn* rather the lord as " he who has power ".[3] Baethgen formulates it : " the lord in relation to his slave is called *ba'al* in so far as he is the possessor of the slave : he is called *'ādhôn* in so far as he can do what he likes with this possession ".[4] Thus the distinction between the words is related to that between δεσπότης and κύριος, and the latter is the counterpart of *'ādhôn*.

Perhaps there is even more evidence in Egyptian for the link between the lordship of the deity over nature, or parts of it, and the spoken expression for it in the concept of the lord. It seems to be the case that the transference of *kurios* to gods because of an indigenous, non-Greek, usage took place independently in Egypt and Syria ; Baudissin's supposition that this use of *kurios* as a divine epithet came from Syria to Egypt, is very improbable.[5] In this he was led astray by the erroneous belief that in Egypt " lord " is " never used for an epithet standing alone or linked with a pronominal suffix",[6] which he bases upon an obviously misunderstood statement of Erman's.[7] In fact the link of *nb* (lord) and (less frequently) *nb.t* (" lady ")

[1] Op. cit. p. 620.

[2] Op. cit. p. 526.

[3] Gesenius-Buhl, s.v. *'ādhôn*. G. Dalman, *Der Gottesname Adonaj und seine Geschichte* (1889), pp. 10 f.

[4] F. Baethgen, *Beiträge zur semitischen Religionsgeschichte* (1888), p. 41.

[5] Baudissin, op. cit. ii, pp. 266-9.

[6] Op. cit. p. 266.

[7] Op. cit. p. 267, n. 1.

not only with a genitive, but also with a personal suffix, is " the normal and continuous usage ". " The use, with a suffix of the first person, ' my lord ' as a mode of address, ' o my lord Re ', ' O King, my Lord ', etc. is naturally of specially frequent occurrence, but *nb* (*nb.t*) is also linked with all other suffixes—' thy lord ', ' his lords ', ' our lord ', ' your lady ', etc." [1] Thus the use of *kurios*, found in Egypt from the first century B.C. (*vide supra*, p. 18, line 4 ff.), corresponds to an old indigenous usage, by the transference of which into Greek, in accordance with Greek style, the personal suffix came to be omitted.[2]

Thus *kurios* [3] linked with a genitive of the sphere of lordship and *kurios* added as an epithet to a divine name, where the personal suffix mostly disappeared in the transference into Greek, are not, in spite of the obvious distinction, to be completely separated.

(*d*) *Its meaning when used of rulers.* We have already seen the earliest examples of *kurios* applied to rulers. We must leave on one side the phrases κύριος βασιλειῶν and κύριος τριακονταετηρίδων (see p. 12, *ad fin.*), taken from Egyptian titles. This is a mode of expression in conformity with foreign usage, alien to Greek sensibilities. The examples cited on pages 18-19 *supra*, for phrases such as *kurios theos*, *kurios basileūs*, *kurios Kaisar* and *theos kai kurios basileūs*, etc., ceased at the latest during the reign of Tiberius (Ditt. Or. 606—ὑπὲρ [τ]η[ς]

---

[1] Information from H. Grapow.

[2] The use of " lord " without genitive or suffix is indeed " relatively infrequent compared with the huge number of instances at all times of the use with genitive or suffix ". It is limited to (*a*) the superior officer, especially in writing letters (where it was replaced by " my lord " since the Middle Kingdom), (*b*) to the King (since the Middle Kingdom), (*c*) the gods, quite often, especially Osiris, since *c.* 500 B.C. On all this see Erman-Grapow, op. cit.

[3] Especially often of Isis (cf. 1049, l. 19 ff.).

τῶν κυρίων Σε[βαστῶν] σωτηρίας—comes from the time of Augustus or Tiberius). These phrases found in the Orient are translations of indigenous usage, and are paralleled by the fact that the *stratēgos* is similarly named (p. 1048, 36 f.) and *ho theos kai kurios* is also used of priestly superiors.[1] In the Semitic sphere we can instance the formula *'ᵃdhôn mᵉlākhîm* of the Ptolemies.[2]

In the imperial epoch, on the other hand, *kurios* occurs not in solemn and detailed formulations but as a brief summary of the emperor's position in unstressed phrases, especially those giving dates.

The oldest example is *Oxyr. Pap.* I, 37, 5 f. : ζ (ἔτους) Τιβερίου Κλαυδίου Κάισαρος τοῦ κυρίου, also a contemporary *ostrakon*.[3] For Nero, *Oxyr. Pap.* II, 246, provides an interesting example—the smallholder dates his appearance by the year Νέρωνος Κλαυδίου Καίσαρος Σεβαστοῦ Γερμανικοῦ Αὐτοκράτορος and uses the same formula in the attestation of his evidence (ll. 11 f., 24 f.) ; but the three certifying officials date according to the year Νέρωνος τοῦ κυρίου, or Νέρωνος Καίσαρος τοῦ κυρίου (ll. 30, 33, 36). This style of dating begins on *ostraka* with Nero, and grew increasingly predominant.[4] In the longer, official, designations of the emperor, *kurios* by itself appears from the time of

---

[1] B.G.U. 1197, I, 1 (5-4 B.C.) ; 1201, 1, (A.D. 2).

[2] Baethgen, op. cit. p. 41.

[3] Deissmann, *Licht vom Osten*, p. 301.

[4] Deissman, loc. cit. and P. Viereck, *Griechische . . . Ostraka zu Strassburg*, i (1923), registers, for Nero, 8 times the longer formula, 15 times Νέρων ὁ κύριος ; for Vespasian 3 times only the name, once the longer formula, 8 times Οὐεσπασιανὸς (Καῖσαρ) ὁ κύριος; for Domitian 8 times only the name, 4-5 times Δομιτιανὸς ὁ κύριος ; 3 times Δομιτιανὸς Καῖσαρ ὁ κύριος ; for Nerva, 3 times Νέρουας (ὁ) κύριος ; for Trajan, once each Τραιανὸς and Τραιονὸς Ἄριστος, 17 times each Τραιανὸς Καῖσαρ ὁ κύριος and Τραιανὸς ὁ κύριος, once Τραιανος Ἄριστος Καῖσαρ ὁ κύριος.

Nero. (*London Papyri*, 280, 6 . . . cf. Ditt. Syll³ 814,
55.) . . . But the addition of *kurios* to the emperor's
full name is more common since the time of Trajan.
Then ἡμῶν is increasingly added to κύριος (Ditt. Or.
677, 1 ff., *Giessen Papyri*, 7, 10 ff., 21 f.). This gradual
infiltration of *kurios* into the imperial names is independent of the increasing degree to which the
emperors assigned, or allowed to be assigned, divine
honours to themselves ; after the reigns of Nero and
Domitian, which marked a zenith in this connexion,
this use of *kurios* does not disappear, nor become less
frequent. Although Domitian's " dominus ac deus
noster " was eschewed after his death, the short formula
with *kurios* and the use of *kurios* as part of the full name
do not disappear from the *ostraka*. Thus a steady
increase of this use of *kurios* is noticeable from the
time of Nero.

Beside this use of the word with the emperor's name,
kurios is also used absolutely, the earliest example being
Acts xxv. 26. . . .[1] The adjective *kuriakos*, meaning
imperial, which is common in bureaucratic usage,
must also be mentioned.[2]

From the beginning of the imperial epoch, however,
the word " dominus " (*kurios*) plays a yet further part.
If we are to believe the formulation of Plutarch,
Cassius was greeted in Rhodes as βασιλεὺς καὶ κύριος
but declined it with the words : οὔτε βασιλεὺς οὔτε
κύριος, τοῦ δὲ κυρίου καὶ βασιλέως φονεὺς καὶ κολαστής
(cf. *supra*, p. 9, line 13 f.) and Brutus mocks similarly
at Caesar, in saying : οἱ δὲ πρόγονοι ἡμῶν οὐδὲ πρᾴους
δεσπότας ὑπέμεινον (cf. *supra*, p. 9, line 15 f.). Here
an oriental-style monarchy is refused under the name of
kurios and *despotēs*. Thus Caesar's heir Augustus refused

---

[1] Examples . . . especially from Ditt. Syll³ 880, 8 (Pizos,
A.D. 202), *Giessen Papyri*, 3, 12 (Hadrian), 7, 21 f., etc.

[2] Examples in Foerster, op. cit. p. 115, n. 3.

to be called " dominus ". Suetonius says : [1] " Domini
appellationem ut maledictum et opprobrium semper
exhorruit. Cum spectante eo ludos pronuntiatum
esset in mino : O dominum aequum et bonum!
et universi quasi de ipso dictum exultantes com-
probassent, et statim manu vultuque indecoras
adulationes repressit et insquenti die gravissimo
corripuit edicto ; dominumque se posthac appellari
ne a liberis quidem aut nepotibus suis vel serio vel
ioco passus est, atque eius modi blanditias etiam inter
ipsos prohibuit." Similar is the attitude of Tiberius,
of whom Dio Cassius (57, 8, 2) has passed down the
saying : δεσπότης μὲν τῶν δούλων, αὐτοκράτωρ δὲ τῶν
στρατιωτῶν, τῶν δὲ δὴ λοιπῶν πρόκριτός εἰμι. In these passages " lord " is a very definite concept of an absolute
position of a monarch, which also has a legally intelligible aspect.

The special factor in the Roman imperial epoch,
however, is that, under a concealing constitutional
mantle, what resulted was an absolute monarchy, for
the protagonists of which the Orient has always
used the expression " lord ". The scene reported by
Suetonius under Augustus has already shown how
strongly the word for this was already in the air at
Rome. The exposition given above of the emer-
gence of the word *kurios* as a brief expression for the
emperor shows how, despite the official repulse of it
on the part of most emperors, the word " lord "
nevertheless established itself slowly but surely, but
shows at the same time that in these phrases it was not
spoken in " high tones ". With emperor-worship the
noun *kurios*, like the adjective *kuriakos*, has, in the
first instance, nothing in common. There is no text
in which *kurios* applied to a Roman emperor denotes
by itself that the emperor is god. The imperial priest

[1] *Augustus*, 53.

is practically never called *hiereūs tou kuriou*.[1] So too with the formula for the oath to the emperor,[2] with coin inscriptions and acclamations.[3] On the private house-altars of Hadrian in Miletus, which apparently stood once " in every citizen's-house in Miletus ", *kurios* is not found.[4] *Kurios* applied to the emperor has nothing to do with the divine predicate discussed above.

The difficulty lies in another sphere. Though the emperor is not *kurios* as god, he can yet, as *kurios*, be god. In the epigram to Augustus—

Καίσαρι ποντομέδοντι καὶ ἀπείρων κρατέοντι
Ζανί, τῷ ἐκ Ζανὸς πατρός, Ἐλευθερίῳ
δεσπότᾳ Εὐρώπας τε καὶ Ἀσίδος, ἄστρῳ ἁπάσας
Ἑλλάδὸς, [ὃς] σωτ[ὴ]ρ Ζεὺς ἀν[έ]τ[ει]λ[ε] μέγας

(C.I.G. 4923) all the predicates are equally steeped in a kind of religious air : as Zeus rules over all, so is Augustus ποντομέδων and ἀπείρων κρατέων ; and as Helios shines over all parts of the earth, so is Augustus

---

[1] Foerster, op. cit. p. 103. To the exception named there in n. 1, Le Bas and Waddington, op. cit. no. 2606 is relevant (Palmyra A.D. 263).

[2] Foerster, 114 f.

[3] *Kurios* occurs seldom on coins, and apparently not before the second century A.D. Instances have been collected by B. Pick in the *Journal International d'Archéologie Numismatique*, i (1898), pp. 451-63. W. Wruck, *Die syrische Provinzialprägung von Augustus bis Trajan* (1931), gives no instance of *Kurios*, nor does P. L. Strack, *Untersuchungen zur römischen Reichsprägung des II Jahrhunderts*, vol. i (1931), vol. ii (1933), gives one for " dominus ". In Hadrian's second year appears in Alexandria the coin inscription *ΤΡΑΙΑΝΟΣ ΣΕΒΑΣΤΟΣ ΠΑΤ ΚΥ* and in Gallienus' tenth another with, *ΔΕΚΑΕΤΗΡΙΣ ΚΥΡΙΟΥ* (J. Vogt, *Die alexandrinischen Münzen*, ii, pp. 40, 155. Most coins show *kurios* in acclamations, in which it also occurs in Suetonius' *Domitian*, 13, Dio Cassius 72, 20, 2 (of Commodus), *Oxyr. Pap.* I, 41, 3, 11, 20, 30 (third to fourth century A.D.).

[4] T. Wiegand, *Milet*, I, 7 (1924), pp. 350 ff., nos. 290-7.

lord over the then known world. Still clearer an expression of divinity, which is given with the universality of the sphere of lordship, is the inscription of honour for Nero—ὁ τοῦ παντὸς κόσμου κύριος Νέρων [1] ... and of Antoninus Pius we have : ἐγὼ μὲν τοῦ κόσμου κύριος, ὁ δὲ νόμος θαλάσσης.[2] The mental atmosphere behind this is shown in the homage paid by Tiridates to Nero : in Naples he greets him as *despotēs* and expresses *proskunēsis* towards him, in Rome he solemnly declares : ἐγώ, δέσποτα, Ἀρσάκου μὲν ἔκγονος, Οὐολογαίσου δὲ καὶ Πακόρου τῶν βασιλέων ἀδελφός, σὸς δὲ δοῦλός εἰμι. καὶ ἦλθόν τε πρὸς σὲ τὸν ἐμὸν θεόν, προσκυνήσων σε ὡς καὶ τὸν Μίθραν, καὶ ἔσομαι τοῦτο ὅ τι ἂν σὺ ἐπικλώσῃς (decree)· σὺ γάρ μοι καὶ Μοῖρα καὶ Τύχη.[3] Although *kurios* is not used here, he who is *Moira* and *Tuchē* for another man, is his lord. Tacitus, *Annals* II, 87, clearly shows a link between "dominus" and divinity in saying of Tiberius : "acerbeque increpuit eos, qui divinas occupationes ipsumque dominum dixerant". But in one place a "dominus" spoken in high tone is applied to the emperor, and indeed at his own instigation : Domitian not only expressed pleasure at the acclamation in the theatre "domino et dominae feliciter",[4] but he let official letters begin with "dominus et deus noster hoc fieri iubet".[5]

It may be that Caligula had already anticipated him in this formula ; [6] about Aurelian we have coins bearing the inscription "dominus et deus (natus)"— though from a provincial site.[7] It is doubtful whether

[1] Ditt. Syll³ 814, 31.

[2] Justinian, *Digest*, 14, 2, 9, Caracalla is ὁ γῆς καὶ θαλάσσης δεσπότης, I.G. XII, 3, 100.

[3] Dio Cassius 63, 1, 2 ff., especially 63, 2, 4, and 63, 5, 2.

[4] Suetonius, *Domitian*, 13, 1.

[5] Ibid. 13, 2.   [6] . . . Foerster, op. cit. p. 104.

[7] W. Kubitschek in *Numismatische Zeitschrift*, xlviii (New Series VIII) (1915), pp. 167-78.

in the case of Domitian's formula the Greeks wrote *kurios* for " dominus ", and not rather *despotēs*.[1] Statius and Martial give many instances of " dominus " and " dominus et deus ".[2] We have a poem of Martial's in which he disassociates himself from his earlier custom of calling Domitian " dominus et deus ".[3] The two titles are not an hendiadys [4] but hang most closely together. It is precisely because " dominus " here denotes the position of the ruler *vis-à-vis* his subjects [5] that the bearer of this title also styles himself " deus ". Neither of the two titles may here be omitted. The thought which they convey may be evidenced by Domitian's great predecessor, Caesar, who answered a soothsayer who announced an unfavourable omen : " futura laetiora, cum vellet ".[6] It is the same outlook that is expressed by Tiridates before Nero: " dominus " pronounced thus binds a man as God binds him, and if he allows himself to be so bound he must give up his being bound to God, while he who so binds him must take the place of divinity or fate.

It is doubtful, however, whether *kurios*, applied to the emperor, normally had this heightened meaning. The steady increase of the use of *kurios* described above can only be explained if it was in general not used in this sense. Thus Tertullian appropriately distinguishes between " dominus " and " dominus " : " dicam plane imperatorem dominum, sed more

---

[1] Dio Cassius 67, 4, 7.

[2] F. Sauter, *Der Römische Kaiserkult bei Martial und Statius*, pp. 31-40.

[3] X. 72—p. 31 in Sauter.

[4] Lietzmann, *Römerbrief*, on X, 9.

[5] Martial X, 72 : " non est hic dominus, sed imperator ", shows the legal meaning of " dominus " even here, where Martial disassociates himself from the formula " dominus et deus noster ". Cf. Sauter, p. 39, *ad fin.*

[6] Suetonius, *Julius Caesar*, 77.

communi, sed quando non cogor, ut dominum dei vice dicam." [1]

It is not surprising that in the *Acta* of Christian martyrs the opposition to the absolutist claims by the Roman state which sweep away the claims of God also appears in the form that the " dominus noster imperator " is contrasted with the " dominus meus, rex regum et imperator omnium gentium ",[2] but the use of " rex " and " imperator " beside " dominus " shows that it was not a question of the title of " lord " but of the religious claim of the state, in rejecting which the Christians had to show their loyalty to God and the State. In contrast to this stood the *sicarii*, who rejected the emperor as such as their overlord, and therefore refused to call him *despotēs*.[3] With the Christian martyrs religion came up against religion, with the *sicarii*—in the light of Matt. xxii. 21—politics against politics. Since they were excused from the duty of joining in emperor-worship, it was not a question of " lord " pronounced in high tones. The content of *kurios* applied to the emperor could vary greatly, according to the context or the inner disposition of the user of the word : in one of the pagan *Acta Martyrum*, *Oxyr. Pap.* I, 33, the condemned Appian, who calls the Emperor *turannos*, addresses him with a further request as *kurie Kaisar* (III, 1) ; on the other hand, on the lips of Tiridates (*supra*, p. 32, line 8 ff.) the address *despota* expresses the full religious veneration which he then showed and expressed, to Nero. Moreover, the Jews, who rejected the imperial cult, none-the-less consecrated a synagogue ὑπὲρ σωτηρίας τῶν κυρίων ἡμῶν Καισάρων Αὐτοκρατόρων Λ. Σεπτιμίου Σεουήρου Εὐσεβοῦς

---

[1] *Apologeticus*, 34.

[2] *Akten der scilitanischen Märtyrer*, ed. R. Knopf, *Ausgewählte Märtyrerakten* (1913), p. 33.

[3] Josephus, B.J. II, 188 : VII, 418.

Περτίνακος Σεβαστοῦ κτλ.[1] This shows incidentally, how empty the word Σεβαστός, which originally expressed the religious worth of the emperor, had become even by A.D. 197, but it shows especially that the Jews did not hesitate to address their rulers as οἱ κύριοι ἡμῶν.

[1] R. Cagnat, *Inscriptiones graecae ad res Romanas pertinentes III* (1906), 1106.

4

III. THE OLD TESTAMENT NAME FOR GOD

1. *The name for God in the LXX*

In the LXX the word κύριος, meaning God, is only an actual translation where it reproduces 'ādhôn or (in the Kᵉthîbh) 'ᵃdhônāi. As a rule it occurs as a clear periphrasis for the divine name Yahweh, roughly expressing what in the basic passage means the name or the use of the name. That this cannot be completely carried through is obvious from the changing over from the name to the general concept, and from the fact that in the Bible itself, as in ordinary conversation, κύριος is by no means confined to being a designation for God. It corresponds rather to the Hebrew 'ādhôn, used just as much of men, e.g. in the respectful term of address 'ᵃdhônî (in the plural 'ᵃdhônāi—Gen. xix. 2) which occurs 192 times, as of God. It is also used regularly (15 times) to translate baʿal when it occurs in its non-religious meaning of " owner ".[1] The same is true of gᵉbhîr " master " (Gen. xxvii. 29, 37) and of the Aramaic mārē' (used also of God) in Dan. ii. 47, iv. 16, 21, v. 23, and shallîṭ " ruler " (Dan. iv. 14). On the other hand, where baʿal means a heathen divinity, the LXX treats the word either as a proper name (ὁ or ἡ) βάαλ, or interprets it by εἴδωλον (Jer. ix. 13 ; II Chron. xvii. 3, xxviii. 2) or αἰσχύνη (I Kings xviii. 19, 25). Thus in the sphere of religion the designation κύριος or ὁ κύριος is confined to the true God and so corresponds (except for unimportant periphrases in metaphorical language) almost

[1] Cf. Gen. xlix. 23 ; Exod. xxi and xxii (11 times), Judges xix. 22 f. ; Isa. i. 3 ; Job. xxxi. 39.

regularly—to be precise, 6,156 times—to the divine
name *YHWH* in all its punctuations, and when followed
by *ṣᵉbhā'ôth*, or shortened to *yāh*. Only by way of exception are the Hebrew terms for God translated as κύριος
—'*ēl* 60 times, '*elôah* 23 times, '*elôhîm* 193 times,
'*elôhê ṣᵉbhā'ôth* 3 times. The phrases κύριος θεός, κύριος ὁ
θεός and ὁ κύριος θεός mostly indicate a masoretic
YHWH with or without the apposition '*elôhîm*. Only
in Jer. xv. 11 (in the vocative) is *YHWH* translated
by δεσπότης ; otherwise δέσποτα κύριε occasionally
reproduces '*adhônāi YHWH* (Gen. xv. 2 (Swete) and
8 ; Jer. i. 6, iv, 10), which is otherwise usually translated by κύριος κύριος.

The presence or absence of the article before κύριος
seems not to be without significance for the understanding of the meaning of the Greek, however
arbitrary the scribes must be admitted to have been.
For, being a free periphrasis for *YHWH*, κύριος ought
in some sense to be a pointer to the basic word, and
the use of the article should be a good means of telling
whether or not it denotes the singular nature of the
name. Unfortunately the tradition gives us no clear
picture in this respect, but as the use of the article
with θεός in the LXX betrays a certain amount of
method,[1] it may be supposed that the same is true of
κύριος, at least in the case of some of the translators.
At any rate κύριος without the article preserves the
character of the Hebrew basic word as a proper name
more clearly than the form ὁ κύριος which, like
εὐεργέτης or σωτήρ, merely denotes a title.

The consensus of the translators in using this title

---

[1] Baudissin, op. cit. i, p. 441 f. As a general rule κύριος without the article is only used as a designation for God, and occurs
more often in the nominative than in the other cases, where the
article may be thought of as being due to a Hebrew *lᵉ* or '*ēth*.
Cf. Baudissin, op. cit. i, pp. 17 ff.

" lord " or " the lord " for *YHWH* is not completely explained by the supposition that they used some uniform prototype. Especially is this so if one supposes that this prototype in the *Qᵉrê* was '*ᵃdhônāi*, which is common in the final masoretic edition of the Bible text. One would then have to suppose that there was an early form of this tradition spread abroad long before the Christian era in the transcriptions written in Greek—ἀντιγραφαί as Origen probably called them—in which ἀδωναι was substituted for the divine name.[1] But the uncertainty of this hypothesis leaves scope for the other no less uncertain supposition that the Greek translators, from the knowledge of the being of the Old Testament God which was common in Hellenistic Judaism, in free creativeness and making use of the existing usage of κύριος as a divine epithet, used κύριος as a periphrasis for the name of God. In any case there is good reason to suppose that '*ᵃdhônāi* as *Qᵉrê* first came into use as a result of the Greek text, and even as *Kᵉthîbh* seems to have infiltrated relatively late into the Bible text, so that it can only be regarded with reserve, especially in the prophetic books, as being the actual expression of the writers.[2]

Thus the rights and wrongs of the use of κύριος as the Old Testament name for God will not so much be made clear from the use of '*ādhôn* or '*ᵃdhônāi* as from an examination of the reason for and essence of the use of the name *YHWH* in the basic text.

[1] So F. Wutz, *Die transkriptionen von der LXX bis zu Hieronymus*, pp. 145 f.

[2] This is the result of the extensive researches of Baudissin, *Kyrios*, especially vol. ii, p. 305. He infers from the form δέσποτα κύριε for the masoretic '*ᵃdhônāi YHWH* that the translator knew neither the masoretic pronunciation '*ᵃdhônai* '*ᵉlôhîm* nor '*ᵃdhônāi* for the simple *YHWH* (vol. i, p. 523).

2. " Lord " as a designation for Yahweh

The periphrasis " Lord " has undeniably been of as great significance in the history of the Bible and the effect of its message as has the use of the sacred name in the basic passage. Its function has not been completely identical with that, but has overlapped to such an extent that the content of the texts, equally directed towards the fundamental aim of the recognition of divine power, can speak with a telling effect.

'ᵃdhônāi and 'ādhôn differ in that the former (distinguished by the afformative) is reserved for sacred use whereas the simpler 'ādhôn can also be used of human leadership. 'ādhôn is used in the O.T. as the commonest expression for the possessor of power over men (Ps. xii. 5 : of the King, Jeremiah xxii. 18, xxxiv. 5,[1] less frequently over things (Gen. xlv. 8 ; Ps. cv. 21 bayith—which includes men). It is closely linked to ba'al, " possessor ", the stress being significantly less on the legal than on the emotional aspects, as may be inferred from the mode of address 'ᵃdhônî—" my lord "—which is also preferred to ba'al in legally defined relationships of allegiance.[2] It is the term used by the slave to his owner (e.g. Gen. xxiv. 12 ; Exod. xxi. 5) or by the wife to her lord (e.g. Gen. xviii. 12). But it is also usual in the language of the court ('ᵃdhônî hammelekh, e.g. I Sam. xxvi. 17) of adoration (e.g. Num. xi. 28 ; Gen. xxxi. 35) and of common politeness as enjoined by custom (Gen. xxiii. 6 ; Judges iv. 18).

A peculiarity occurs in the secular use of the word in that it often assumes plural forms and suffixes where

---

[1] The cry Hôy 'ādhôn has a formal analogy in the Phoenician Adonis-lament αἴαι Ἄδωνιν, cf. W. W. Count Baudissin, Adonis and Esmun (1911), p. 91.

[2] Ba'ᵃlî occurs only in Hos. ii. 18.

it is not referring to a plurality of persons.[1] Since the
same happens with *ba'al* (e.g. Joshua i. 3) one might
look for the solution in the need for the raising of the
expression to the all embracing level of the conception.[2]
The only difficulty here is the lengthening of the " a "
in *'ᵃdhônāi*, which shows itself to be not due to the pause
and can therefore only be a specially chosen characteristic of the word in its function of giving a name, and
epithet, to God. The conjecture that this is not an
afformative, as the Masoretic text describes it, but a
part of the root, and that the word is borrowed from
some non-semitic language,[3] considerably exaggerates
the philological value of the Masoretic text, while
Punic texts show clearly the pronominal nature of the
suffix.[4] On the other hand, *'ᵃdhônāi* also occurs in
we-texts (e.g. Ps. xliv. 24) so that the interpretation of
it as possessive—" my Lord "—in the Bible texts is
not always tenable without presupposing a formal
petrification of an originally intended vocative to a
nominative.[5] Granted this presupposition, it may be
assumed, without denying the philological possibility
mentioned above, that *'ᵃdhônāi* as a designation for
God is derived from a private prayer-form, as is in fact

[1] Typical is *'ᵃdhônîm qāsheh*—" an austere master ", Isa.
xix, 4.

[2] Gesenius-Kautsch, *Hebräische Grammatik* (1909), § 124, i.

[3] H. Bauer and P. Leander, *Historische Grammatik der Hebr.
Sprache*, i (1922), § 2, h, 29, t. *'ādhôn* would then be a " secondary
singular ", § 61, i, a (p. 469). The word is not in all semitic
languages, but only found among Israelites and Phoenicians—
that too suggests borrowing.

[4] Cf. e.g. *'ᵃdhônî Ba'alshāmēm* (Umm-el-'Awâmîd, *Corpus
Inscriptionum Semiticarum*, ed. E. Renan I, 1 (1881), 7, l. 7;
M. Lidzbarski, *Altsemitische Texte*, i (1907), p. 22). Further
material in Baudissin, *Adonis and Esmun*, p. 66.

[5] For the transition of the vocative into other cases, Baudissin
in *Kyrios*, ii, pp. 35 ff. compares *rabbî* as title, the Syriac *mârî*,
also the Accadian *belti*.

often to be found in the Masoretic text.[1] The lengthening of the " a " must be due to the Masoretes' desire
to mark the word as sacred by this small change.
The fact that they were probably also keen on the
circumstance that *'adhônāi* has four Hebrew letters
corresponding to the tetragram,[2] perhaps explains why
the " my-form " established itself instead of the " our-
form " *'adhônênû* found in Ps. viii. 2, 10, cxlvii. 5,
cxxxv. 5, etc.[3]

When used of Yahweh, *'ādhôn*, like *melekh*, connotes
His sovereign power. It is a title which corresponds
to His being, only seldom does it point to His position
as Lord of a district—as probably in the appositional
linking of the words " The Lord Yahweh " in Exod.
xxiii. 17, xxxiv. 23,[4] where the theme is harvest festivals. As *'abhîr Yiśrā'ēl*, " the strength of Israel " (cf.
Gen. xlix. 24) he is called *'ādhôn* in Isa. i. 24. From
this it may be inferred that Isaiah in other passages
too [5] may only use the word in this sense, if it really
does belong to his own vocabulary at all.[6] But in
general the O.T. texts about Yahweh as *'ādhôn* have
already passed beyond the conception of Yahweh as
Lord of the land and people, and more or less clearly
presuppose the prophetic faith in Yahweh as lord of
all. The form " Lord of the whole earth " (Mic. iv.

---

[1] The list in Baudissin, *Kyrios*, p. 60, shows 55 cases, with 31
'adhônāi yahweh.

[2] Cf. A. Geiger, *Urschrift und Übersetzungen der Bibel* (2nd edn.
1928), p. 262.

[3] Baudissin, op. cit. ii, p. 27, considers *'adhônênû* as derived from
'adhônāi.

[4] Cf. Buber, op. cit. p. 124.

[5] The full-sounding phrase *Hā 'ādhôn Yahweh ṣebhā'ôth* is confined to the Book of Isaiah, occurring twice in the audition-
formula (i. 24, xix. 4) 3 times in free introductions of woes.

[6] The tradition is not clear ; cf. *Biblia Hebraica*, ed. R. Kittel
(3rd edn. 1929) on the passages cited in the previous note.

13 ; Zech. iv. 14, vi. 5 ; Ps. xcvii. 5 ; Joshua iii. 11
and 13) shows most clearly how the meaning has risen
to be comprehensive. Thus this will also be the meaning when *ādhôn* stands in isolation (only Ps. cxiv. 7),[1]
and there can be no question about the " total "
meaning for the lengthened form *'adhônāi* as well.

The questionability of the *Kᵉthîbh 'adhônāi* has
already been recalled, page 38 above. But the fact
is that this *Kᵉthîbh*, even where it can be considered the
foundation of the text, as in Isa. vi, in the main does
its best, like the *Qᵉrê* derived from it, to avoid mentioning the name of God. In Isa. vi. 11, the prophet
uses the vocative *'ᵃdhônāi* spontaneously under the
undiminished impression of the nearness of God's
majesty, and one might ask whether *'ᵃdhônî* was not
used there. But the desire to avoid mentioning the
name, since man is confronted by the majesty that
" fills the whole earth " is as clear in that passage as
almost anywhere. On the other hand, the use of
'ᵃdhônāi at the beginning of Isa. vi. 1 and 8,[2] suggests
that here there is an exemplary desire to instil into the
reader the thoughts expressed in the seraphim-hymn
by a choice of words to match the prophet's reverence.
That is also probably the significance of the phrase so
frequent in Ezekiel, *'ᵃdhônāi Yahweh* or *Yahweh 'ᵃdhônāi*
(212 times according to Baudissin) : it serves to some
extent as an elucidation of the name as an expression
for the divine majesty, and the transition of the stress
from name to title is undeniable. Thus the *Kᵉthîbh's*
use of *'adhônāi* seems to have inaugurated a development of the technique of the tradition which finally
resulted in the *Qᵉrê's* complete exclusion of the divine

---

[1] *Hā 'ādhôn* in Mal. III, 1 can also, despite Baudissin's hesita-
tions (*Kyrios*, vol. ii, p. 305) be interpreted thus.

[2] The *Biblia Hebraica* note on this passage says that c. 100 MSS.
read *Yahweh!*

name from the text. Such desires were probably strongly fostered by the use of the courtesy title " my lords " in the story of Sodom (Gen. xviii-xix), so significantly valued by the Masoretes,[1] for the visitors to Abraham and Lot, among whom (as the reader gathers from the context) was " the judge of the whole earth " (xviii. 25) who had " come down " (xviii. 21).

The substitution of *'ᵃdhônāi*, cautiously adopted by the *Kᵉthibh*, and carried through by the *Qᵉrê* to the complete exclusion of the pronunciation of the divine name, gives us nothing less than a summary exegesis of the entire Holy Scripture of Israel. Together with the LXX's use of κύριος it betokens an act of unlimited significance in the history of religion. The considerations which prepared the way for it and led to its adoption cannot be reconstructed with a high degree of certainty (*vide infra*, p. 59, line 5 ff.). Not even does the question touched upon above (*vide infra*, p. 72, *ad fin.*), whether the LXX or its precursors gave the first impulse, admit of a satisfactory answer. A definite missionary impulse is unlikely to be the reason, at any rate the chief one, since the active missionary epoch of Judaism had not yet dawned when the LXX was finished, and was already over when the last Masoretes set their seal to the *Qᵉrê*. But the missionary activity has left many traces in the text of the LXX.

An enormous missionary power lies in the last verses of Ps. cxxxiv (Heb. and Eng. cxxxv), when, after the House of Israel, Aaron and Levi, the φοβούμενοι τὸν κύριον, are also called upon to praise the Lord of all. It stands beyond all doubt that this expansion

---

[1] The words addressed to the three (xviii. 3) are pointed as a designation of God, because God must be one of them. The two other men are greeted by Lot in secular style (xix. 2). In the end the mythical *motif* of the three men fades away, and it is a question of Yahweh alone (xix. 18).

of the terminology used for expressing God, theologically due to the prophets, played a most important part in the spreading of the O.T. message. If it signified a relaxation of its historical ties, it was no severance of them. If it diminished its numinous power over Israel, it surrendered to a decisive point the national character of the canon, and thereby interpreted its deepest meaning. The God to whom the canon bears witness is called " Lord " because He is there shown to be the sole exerciser of power over the universe and all mankind, as the creator of the world and disposer of life and death. Thus the term " Lord " conveys a summary of the faith of the O.T. It is the completely successful attempt to express what God is, what is the practical significance for mankind of the holy, i.e. the advent of a personal will, and to express this with almost the same pregnancy and inevitability as is demanded by the special characteristics of the term *Yahweh*.

3. *The name Yahweh as a concept of experience*

The O.T. faith in God is grounded in historical experience and developed in continuous contact with history. The clearest expression of this fact is the use of the name Yahweh in speaking of, and calling upon, God. This name, like every name for God, is a concept of experience and as such, through its concrete and individual content, differs in degree from general concepts verging upon the abstract such as '*ēl*, '*elôah*, and '*elôhîm*, and from the designation of honour '*ādhôn*. It denotes not just any divinity, but a definite, unambiguous, divine person. It fills the terms " God " and " Lord " with so strongly numinous a content, that the final result is that it completely overshadows their general meaning, so that " God " is no longer an appellation of multifarious application and " Lord "

comes to mean " the Lord of all ". It follows that the
general concepts, although infrequent in the canon,
can often be used as synonyms for Yahweh, and
'adhônāi itself replaces them. They have absorbed the
significance of the personal name, they have become
experimental concepts of unambiguous form. Thus
the understanding of the translators must orientate
upon such sentences as " the Lord is God " (I Kings
xviii. 39 ; cf. Joshua xxiv. 15) or " the Lord is His
name " (Exod. xv. 3) if the clear direction of the Bible
terminology towards the person of Yahweh is to be
faithfully retained. For the basic text does not say
that " God " or " Lord " is a name, but in the naming
any other word than Yahweh is expressly excluded.
" Yahweh is His name ", or " Yahweh of hosts
(*Yahweh ṣebhā'ôth*) is His name "—these are phrases
common in hymnody.[1] They ensure first and foremost that the personal designation of God, with a vivid
consciousness of its extent, has been directed to a very
definite experience of the divine. God thus named is
for His confessors as for others a figure strongly defined,
the *numen praesens* in person. " To call Yahweh by
name " (*qārā' beshēm Yahweh*, e.g. Isa. lxv 1) means to
owe allegiance to, and hold oneself ready to encounter,
this figure.[2] Only he who " knows Him not ", as the
heathen, (Ps. lxxix. 6 ; Jer. x. 25) can achieve nothing
with the name of Yahweh, which is the addressible
" Thou " of the man of prayer,[3] symbol of all the

[1] Cf. the complete indication of the passages concerned in Grether,
op. cit. p. 55. On their meaning see Buber-Rosenzweig, op. cit. p. 335.

[2] For the " de-magicing " of the phrase, cf. Grether, op. cit.
pp. 21-2.

[3] This may be the meaning of the almost untranslatable word
we'attāh-hû' in Ps. cii. 28, a stammer of " Thou art He " with the
accent entirely on " Thou ". *hû'* only fills up the tone as in
'anî-hû', Isa. xli. 4, etc., cf. Job iii. 19. It follows that all these
passages are of no relevance to the derivation of the word Yahweh.

power and will of God. In the language of doctrine this may also be expressed by saying " *shēm* is always the name of God as He is revealed ".[1]

Thus wherever this proper name for God occurs in the texts, it creates quite independently of its meaning, but as a result solely of its nature as a concept of experience, an indissoluble link between religion and history, the history in which the use of this name originated and developed in the fashion indicated above. The name Yahweh, no matter if and when it was used before (*vide infra*, p. 50) was the framework of revelation in the religious foundation of Moses and points back implicitly to this historical confrontation of God and man and all that resulted therefrom. It is as unspiritual as the one designation for God well can be, and it provides practically no opportunities for speculation about the divine, but it recalls [2] silently and permanently a vitalising proclamation of God which was known to have happened in the early age of the people of Israel, and reminds us of encounters in the lives of prophetic men who were called to declare, as Yahweh's mouthpieces, in full authority, " Thus has Yahweh spoken ". The use of the name makes visible the essential and ineradicable features of the picture of God which is painted by the biblical tradition in the portrayal of the inner history of the people of God and the spiritual moulding of its religious leaders up to the inevitable showing forth of divine reality. The deeply-felt pathos, the searing honesty of O.T. piety, is rooted in the message about Yahweh, in whose clearly defined divine personality, in whose insistent will man finds a norm and criterion for life and the

---

[1] Grether, op. cit. p. 18 ; cf. pp. 159 ff.

[2] Cf. the synonym *zēkher* for *shēm*, e.g. Exod. iii. 15 and the cultic phrase " to bring the name into remembrance " (Exod. xxiii. 13).

world, now cowering in a feeling of creaturely dependence before the Holy, now satiated with rapt gazing at the figure (Ps. xvii. 15) in whom all salvation lies guaranteed. " The fact that in Yahweh the features of the personality are so incomparably great is of the essence of his value and his superiority over all the gods of the peoples." [1]

4. The Foundation of Moses

The religion of the O.T. as the cult of Yahweh is a *founded* religion. Moses' proclamation of the divine name did not mean only " a yahwistic reform of Canaanite animism " [2] but a new beginning of religious life to which no theories of evolution or balancing out can do justice. True, both ancient and modern traditions include full reports of a history of faith in Yahweh in the pre-Mosaic generations of the patriarch. The migration of Abraham from Mesopotamia to Canaan was undertaken out of obedience to Yahweh, and the rejection of the service of other gods (Joshua xxiv. 2 f. ; Gen. xii. 8, xxxv. 2 ; Judith v. 5-7). The kernel of these traditions—the significance of which for salvation appears with especial impressiveness in Gen. xii. 1 ff.—must be confined to the message that religious movements played a certain, though perhaps not decisive part in the obscure incidents in the pre-history of the tribes of Israel.[3] The account of the J source, which, unlike E and P, assumes that in the very earliest age of man the name of Yahweh was used

[1] R. Otto, *Das Gefühl des Überweltlichen* (1932), p. 269.

[2] G. Van der Leeuw, *Phänomenologie der Religion* (1933), p. 581. For the concept " founder ", *vide* pp. 618 ff. The functions of witness, prophet, teacher, even theologian, are comprised in the biblical tradition about Moses, of which the legendary extent vouches for his position as acknowledged founder.

[3] Cf. R. Kittel, *Geschichte des Volkes Israel*, i (1923), pp. 289 f.

(as a result of some primitive revelation) for calling upon God (Gen. iv. 26) cannot, in view of the lack of precise statements such as Hos. xii. 10 (" I am Yahweh, thy God from the land of Egypt "; cf. xiii. 4) or Exod. vi. 3 (" By my name Yahweh, am I not known to them ", P), seriously question the historical value of the tradition of the founding of the worship of Yahweh by Moses. The attempt to fit the name of Yahweh, and especially the observation taught in Gen. iv. 26, into pre-history as evidence of an innate conception of the creator and Lord of the world is, from an historical standpoint, no more than a faint echo of the scarcely comprehensible fact that the divine name already existed, and had some prehistoric location somewhere before Moses introduced it to the children of Israel (*vide infra*, pp. 50, *ad fin.* ff.).

It was in the age of Moses that the worship of Yahweh enters the sphere of history—if it was not then that it first came to life itself. Then first, at any rate, it begins to have visible effects as the religion of a nationally conscious federation of the tribes of Israel,[1] as the cause of political actions and the sovereign norm of the pattern of life. The history of the foundation, it is true, is itself shrouded in a saga, not completely free of legendary elements, about a theophany vouchsafed to Moses. As a result of the revelation received, Moses became the founder of the loyalty, sworn in the Covenant, of a league of Israelite clans, to the commanding and protecting God Yahweh. The religious inheritance of these tribes—which previously seems to have embraced a manifold variety of divine beings,[2]

[1] The name Israel, which occurs as early as 1223 B.C. on a *stēlē* of Merneptah, does not presuppose the worship of Yahweh, but aptly indicates its basic impulse if the most likely derivation, " God fights, or strives ", is correct. Cf. W. Caspari, *Zeitschrift für Semitistik*, iii (1924), pp. 194 ff.

[2] Cf. A. Alt, *Der Gott der Väter* (1929), pp. 3 ff.

each with his own *hieros logos*—was from now on strongly directed towards the concretely-formed reality, perceived by Moses. As a result, a previously unknown outlook now dominated all the utterances of the "people of Yahweh" (Judges v. 11) the trust in the guiding will and power of the God who was subject to no natural limitations, who in the most critical moment of the exodus of Moses' troop out of Egypt had revealed His transcendent majesty as He hurled horse and rider into the sea (Exod. xv. 21).[1] It is from the time of Moses that the tradition of a common worship of Yahweh can be dated.[2] The tribes leave Egypt, to honour Him in a festival in the wilderness (Exod. iii. 12 (E), iv. 23 (J), etc.). To this epoch, moreover, belongs the first appearance of God-linked personal names which indicate allegiance to Yahweh : *Yᵉhôshûaʿ* [Joshua] is probably the earliest—if one regards *Yôkhebhedh* [Jochebed], the name of Moses' mother (Exod. vi. 20 (P)) as not derived from Yahweh or as not authentic.[3] Now, too, the "Wars of

---

[1] O. Eissfeldt, *Baal Zephon* . . . (1932), pp. 66 ff. cautiously discusses the possibility that the help experienced was ascribed at first to the "God of this district", later to Yahweh. This hypothesis is only possible under gross misunderstanding of the circumstances of Exod. xv. The hymn about the sea centres on what was a decisive turning point for the whole future of Israel and was reckoned as the rock bottom of her hymnody ; cf. A. Weiser, *Glaube und Geschichte im A.T.* (1931), pp. 3 f. A transposed legend could not attain such significance. It presupposes, moreover, that the revelation of Yahweh came after the Exodus for which there is no evidence.

[2] This has given rise to the thesis that the community-form of the Yahweh-tribes is analogous to the Amphictyonic League in ancient Greece. Cf. A. Alt., R.G.G.², III, 438 f.

[3] The name is missing in Exod. ii. 1, where it ought to occur. Probably it was taken from some other context by P and given to Moses' mother. But cf. M. Noth, *Die israelitischen Personennamen* (1928), p. 111, and H. Bauer, *Z.A.W.*, N.S. x (1933), pp. 92 f.

Yahweh " begin (Num. xxi. 14 ; I Sam. xviii. 17) wars
which groups forming the backbone of the convenant-
league prosecuted in offensives, not always successful,
against Canaanite communities. " Arise O Yahweh,
that their enemies may scatter and they that hate thee
flee before thee " (Num. x. 35) ; so runs the battle
cry, when Yahweh's emblem [1] is carried before, presumably the holy shrine as symbol of the presence of
the God worshipped. Victory is Yahweh's, defeat
means Yahweh's wrath. " Who among the Gods is
like unto thee, Yahweh? Thou art praised as the
fearful one that doeth wonders ! " (Exod. xv. 11.)
With the acceptance of the name of Yahweh began
the religion of Israel as a warlike and exclusive
allegiance to the God who guided, as an active
submission to His will (cf. also Joshua xxiv. 16 ff.).

5. *The provenance of the Divine Name*

Whence came the name of this powerful God?
The tradition in Exodus iii answers " From God's
own mouth "—and thereby shows the ambiguity of
the procedure when the divine expresses itself in the
form of human speech. But was this form merely
created by the founder of the religion, or did he adopt
it from some tradition? No one can answer these
questions with certainty. If the answer to the first is
in the negative, then some sort of probability must be
established in reply to the second ; but that has not
yet been convincingly achieved.

The possibility of a Yahweh outside and before
Israel, which had been raised by a certain discovery

---

[1] This is found as late as Exod. xvii. 15, Yahweh's *nissî* ; but
perhaps the reference is to a throne ; cf. *kesyāh* as *K^ethîbh* in
verse 16.

among Accadian personal names [1] and attracted much attention, has been raised again by texts from Ras Shamra,[2] a Syrian coastal resort which certainly goes back to a date before Moses (1500-1200 B.C.). The circumstance that a divinity *yaw* occurs there, whose name bears an undeniable affinity to the form of *Yahweh* common in proper names, which is also found independently in inscriptions, is scarcely to be explained by the theory that it is a question of philological coincidence,[3] although there is some superficial probability that this may be so. Conjecture could also turn towards Egyptian religion, especially to Amun Re' the " King of the Gods " who resided in Thebes,[4] if it were worth while to trace a religious tradition which might conceivably have bequeathed some inheritance to the Yahweh-tradition or could explain the origin of the name. But such conjectures lead to no settled conclusions.[5]

[1] Cf. the collection of material in J. Hehn, *Die biblische und die babylonische Gottesidee* (1913), pp. 230 ff. ; G. R. Driver, " The Original Form of the Name Yahweh " (*Z.A.W.*, 1928, pp. 7 ff.). Well-attested identity of divine elements in names compounded with Yahweh is rare, and does not as yet extend back beyond the era of the prophets. For the specially suggestive name *Ya'u-bi'di*, see Noth, op. cit. p. 110. [See also J. W. Jack, " The Ras Shamra Tablets ", O. T. Studies No. I (1935).]

[2] Cf. O. Eissfeldt, *Zeitschrift der deutschen Morgenländischen Gesellschaft* (1934), pp. 173 ff. ; R. Dussaud, *Les Textes de Ras Shamra et l'Ancien Testament* (1937).   [3] See Bauer, op. cit. pp. 92 ff.

[4] K. Sethe, *Amun und die acht Urgötter von Hermopolis* (*Abhandlungen*, Berlin Academy, 1929, no. 4), bases his conjecture of an Egyptian precursor of the conception of Yahweh upon passages which connect Yahweh with *rûaḥ* (pp. 119 f.) to which he assigns the very name of Yahweh (see n. 3, p. 56 *infra*). But these passages would have to be more strongly emphasised in the proclamation of Yahweh and to be assignable to an earlier date, to make the idea of Amun's being a precursor acceptable.

[5] There is a collection of further hypotheses, some of them fantastic, in A. Schleiff, *Zeitschrift der deutschen Morgenländischen Gesellschaft* (1936), pp. 683 ff.

The same is true of the so-called "Kenite-hypo-thesis"[1] which has achieved a certain importance as the relatively most concrete filling of the vacuum. Based upon the account of the marriage of Moses with the daughter of Jethro, the priest of the Midianites (Exod. iii. 1—another name is found in ii. 18), and his assistance with the organisation of government among the tribes of Israel (Exod. xviii. 1 ff.), it sup-poses that Yahweh was the God of the nomadic tribe of the Kenites, to which, according to Judges i. 16 (cf. also iv. 11) Moses was bound by oath. This thesis draws a certain amount of support from the traditions connecting Yahweh with the mountain of Sinai (J) or Horeb (E). To it was led the host of Moses, migrating out of Egypt (Exod. xix. 3 f.), there is His *temenos*, His "holy ground" (Exod. iii. 5, J). From there He sets forth with the people for the struggle for Canaan (*bā' missînai*, Deut. xxxiii. 2). Less precisely it is stated in the Song of Deborah (Judges v. 4) that Yahweh went out from Seir, and marched from the field of Edom[2] to wage war. These texts speak of Yahweh as domiciled in the territories bordering upon Canaan to the South—of Elijah too it is reported that he sought and found the presence of Yahweh on Horeb (I Kings xix. 8 ff.). Thus if Yahweh had really been a god of the nomads bivouacking in the open country, then the history of His name would turn up out of the prehistoric past of those tribes.[3]

But to speak with enough certainty to lead to definite

---

[1] First put forward in detail by B. Stade, *Z.A.W.*, xiv (1894), pp. 250 ff., later expressed with great confidence by H. Schmökel, "Jahveh und die Keniter", *Journal of Biblical Literature*, lii (1933), pp. 212 ff.

[2] Note the harmonising gloss in verse 5 : "That is Sinai".

[3] A. Alt, *Der Gott der Väter* (1929), p. 6, n. 2, refers to *'ahiyyû* in Nabatean names in the third century.

conclusions is in every respect denied, and to fill up the gaps with conjectures about Moses' personal contribution to the form of the divine name [1] is completely useless. All we can cling on to is the possibility that the god Yahweh was an object of worship tied to some locality, like many others, so that the foundation by Moses also signified a reformation in the sense that it filled a very old form of epiklesis with new content.

6. *The form and meaning of the name Yahweh*

In these circumstances it would be of great importance to know the original meaning of the name Yahweh, since from that, even though it should not have been always present to the minds of those who spoke and heard it, one could probably arrive at important conclusions about the root and original colour of the view of god entailed in the name. But there are difficulties in the tradition with regard to the mere form of the name which prevent us, or rather ought to prevent us, from reading the word in its full tonal form without the occurrence of objections.

(*a*) There is not even an unambiguous tradition for the make-up of the consonants. The so-called tetragram YHWH, occurring 5,321 times in the O.T., alternates with the digram YH, which occurs 25 times, and the relationship between the short form and the long form is not clear (*vide infra*, p. 57, *ad fin.*). The Elephantine Papyri write YHW, for which— presumably in error—YHH is also found. YHW [2] which also appears epigraphically, occurs in alternation with YW at the beginning of proper names, cf.

---

[1] Cf. Schleiff, op. cit. p. 696.
[2] [The Hebrew consonant W is also used as the vowel Ô or Û.]

Yᵉhôyāqîm, *Yô'ēl*, etc., at the end of names it alternates with YH, cf. *'ēliyyāhû*, *yᵉshaʿyāh*, etc. It is not possible to be certain which of these forms is the original. The earliest known is *YHWH*, which appears on the ninth century *stēlē* of King Mesha of Moab in old semitic script, which completely excludes the doubt which so easily arises in the square script about such ambiguous letters as *YW* and *H*.[1]

This combination of consonants admits neither of a fixed reading nor of an unambiguous interpretation, since even in the Masoretic text the vowels added to the tetragram vary and in any case show themselves to be a foreign addition to the word. Alongside the most frequent form *Yᵉhôwāh* we find, in conjunction with an *'ᵃdhônāi* before or after the tetragram, the reading *Yᵉhôwih*. In old and important manuscripts with tiberian vocalisation (as e.g. in Codex B 19 a Leningradensis (sign L), which is the basis of the third edition of *Biblia Hebraica* by R. Kittel and P. Kahle), we frequently find *Yᵉhwāh* (without a *ḥôlem*),[2] while texts with Babylonian pointing regularly refrain from any vocalisation of the divine name or else follow the tiberian tradition.[3] From this changing situation it must be deduced that the vocalisation is not essential to the word in this or that instance, but denotes that the *Qᵉrê* was periphrastic. *Yᵉhôwāh* was to be read as *'ᵃdhônāi* " Lord of all ", *Yᵉhôwih* as *'ᵉlôhîm*, " God ", *Yᵉhwāh* as *shᵉmā'*, " the name ", with the proper name for god itself disappearing

---

[1] Mesha Inscription, line 18 ; cf. M. Lidzbarski, *Handbuch der nordsemitischen Epigraphik* (1898), pp. 415 and 286 . . . .

[2] J. Fischer, *Biblica*, xv (1934), pp. 50 ff., establishes the pointing *Yᵉhwah* (without *ḥôlem* and with *pathaḥ*) in a scholastic source; *qāmeṣ* is completely unknown in the manuscripts ; cf. *Werden und Wesen des A.T.* (= *Z.A.W.*, Beiheft 66), pp. 198 ff.).

[3] P. Kahle, *Der masoretische Text des A.T. nach der Überlieferung der babylonischen Juden* (1902), p. 11.

out of reading and meditation.[1] It is *shēm hamᵉ-phôrash*, " the expressive name ".[2]

(*b*) Thus attempts to arrive at the original complete form and the inherent meaning of *YHWH* cannot count upon assistance from the biblical tradition, but must depend solely upon philological combinations. Even Exod. iii. 14, as will be seen shortly (p. 61, *ad fin.*) contributes nothing, so that from the very start there must be no expectation that any of the results of such deliberations will attain a degree of certainty sufficient for definite conclusions to serve the interpretation of the usage of *YHWH*. Nevertheless much ingenuity has been devoted to these attempts in pursuing the two possibilities of (1) a basic root *HWH*, (2) a formation upon some other basis.

(*a*) The vowel-less tetragram *YHWH* appears to be either a verbal or a substantival form of the root *YWH*. The most probable hypothesis seems to be a verbal inflexion, especially when account is taken of the report of Theodoret of Cyros,[3] that the Samaritans said 'Ιαβέ and that of Clement of Alexandria,[4] that the name was 'Ιαουε. True, the question immediately arises as to what the subject of the verb might be. On the analogy of many verbal names of persons, e.g. *Yaʿᵃqōbh*, *Yiṣḥāq*, one might think of an *hypocoristicum* which has excluded the element forming the subject of the verbal clause.[5] In that case the intrinsic meaning of the name

[1] When the tetragram appears outside the Canon, e.g. in the Targums, the masoretic editing is taken as authentic.

[2] Geiger, op. cit. p. 264 ; Bousset-Gressmann, op. cit. p. 309, n. 2.

[3] *Quaestio* 15 in Exod. 7 (Migne, 80, p. 244 a, b).

[4] *Strom.* V, 6, 34 : τὸ τετράγραμμον ὄνομα τὸ μυστικόν, ὃ περιέκειντο οἷς μόνοις τὸ ἄδυτον βάσιμον ἦν · λέγεται δὲ 'Ιαουε.

[5] The once widely misunderstood Accadian person's name *jawiilu*, or *jawi-Dagan*, in which *jawi* is not a name but a verb, shows the philological possibility with especial impressiveness. Th. Bauer, *Die Ostkanaanäer* (1928), pp. 56, 61, 63, 74.   (H. Bauer, op. cit. p. 93, still maintains the old interpretation.)

would only be half preserved in the surviving phrase. But although this scheme of name-forming is often used for names of persons linked with gods, for divine names, on the other hand, it cannot be instanced with any certainty, if it were to be proposed that the verbal meaning should be held back in favour of the substantival.

But if *YHWH* is a noun with a prefixed *Y*, its meaning must still depend upon the root *HWH*, which seems to be less at home in Hebrew than in Aramaic. The two meanings that confront us in the O.T. (*a*) " to fall ", and (*b*) " to be ", have so little to do with one another that one does well not to mix them.[1] Job. xxxvii. 6, *hᵉwē' 'ereṣ*, " fall to the earth " corresponds exactly to the Arabic *hawa'*, " to fall ".[2] If *YHWH* is he who " falls ", then lightning or meteors could be meant, and the sphere of a storm-god be given.[3] But if we consider the Aramaic *HWH*, " to be " (cf. Gen. xxvii. 29 *hᵉwēh gᵉbhîr lᵉʾaheykhā;* Isa. xvi. 4), then *YHWH* could mean " he who is ", or " being " personified—which is incidentally much too abstract to carry conviction.

(*β*) Uncertain as these conclusions may be, the other possibility, interpreting *YHWH* from its shorter form (which leaves the root *HWH* less clearly discernible),

---

[1] E. König, *Hebr. und aram- Wörterbuch z.A.T.* (1910), pp. 76 f. s.v. *HWH* attempts a very violent conflation, comparing the Latin cecidit and accidit. He sees the meaning " to be " as a metaphysical spiritualised conception of " to fall ". This is hardly conceivable.

[2] Cf. *hawwāh* (also *hōwāh*) " fall ", in the Psalms *passim*, for the deed which leads to a fall—also metaphorically of folly. [Rev. Islwyn Blythin says the Arabic root ends with a Yôdh, not an Aleph, so points it *haway*.]

[3] The derivation from the Arabic *hwj*, to blow, has a certain significance for Sethe's conjectures (p. 51, n. 4); unfortunately it is not " absolutely certain " (op. cit. p. 120), but is inconclusive, as are all other attempts to find the original meaning.

also leads to no evidence. The shorter form which occurs in the Bible text—chiefly in the liturgical formula $hal^el\hat{u}$-$y\bar{a}h$—is $y\bar{a}h$.[1] In the Elephantine Papyri the divine name occurs as YHW—which out of wilfulness or carelessness occasionally appears as YHH. As a termination of god-linked personal names ($Yirm^ey\bar{a}h\hat{u}$, etc.) the masoretic text expresses it as $y\bar{a}h\hat{u}$ and as $y^eh\hat{o}$ at the beginning of such names (e.g. $Y^eh\hat{o}n\bar{a}th\bar{a}n$) or, with elision as $Y\hat{o}$ (e.g. $Y\hat{o}h\bar{a}n\bar{a}n$).[2] There is further the transcription 'Ιαώ, in numerous, even pre-christian, texts,[3] even though many of these must be excluded as evidence for the biblical name of God, for writers as early as Irenaeus (*Haer.* I, 30, 5) and Origen (*Cels.* VI, 32) recall that 'Iao (or Iaoth, or 'Ιαώ was clearly used by the Gnostics, as a result of borrowing, as the name of a god or *daemon*. Thus YHW can be pronounced either $Y\bar{a}h\hat{u}$ or $Y\bar{a}h\hat{o}$.[4]

(γ) The relation between the short and the long form constitutes an inexplicable problem. If one sees in the short form $y\bar{a}h$, an interjection [5] found also in Arabic, a " god-cry ", this is based on a correct calculation, that proper names originated from a practical desire, namely to be able to call upon someone.[6] But this consideration can contribute nothing to the interpretation in face of the fact that $y\bar{a}h$, as much as

---

[1] Transcribed 'Ια in Origen, *In Celsum*. VI 32, v. l., in Jerome, *Breviarium in Psalmos* on Ps. 146 (Migne 26, p. 1253b), also in Θ.

[2] Inscriptions give similar evidence. Cf. Lidzbarski, op. cit. p. 286.   [3] Diodorus Siculus I, 94, 2.

[4] Jerome, op. cit. on Ps. 8 (p. 838a) also gives evidence for $Yaho$ in a very instructive sentence. " Nomen domini apud Hebraeos quatuor literarum est, yod, he, vau, he, quod proprie dei vocabulum sonat ; et legi potest Iaho, et Hebraei ἄρρητον, id est, ineffabile opinantur."

[5] Driver, op. cit. p. 24.

[6] Cf. Buber, op. cit. p. 236 ; R. Otto, op. cit. conjectures a dervish cry, referring to the $n^ebh\hat{i}$'$\hat{i}m$.

the tetragram, is a name applied to the divine person. The monosyllabic call is completely colourless and constitutes no name, even if one brings in a *hû'* (meaning " he ") to fill it out. A he is no thou.[1] Then the long form, the tetragram, must also be thought of as originating from some kind of learned process,[2] against which is not only the early instances *YHWH* (p. 54, n. 1) but also the inflexions with *-yama* in accadian yahwistic personal names which are based upon the longer form.[3] The possibility that the longer and short forms before us are quite separate words deserves some attention, in view of the difficulty of explaining the relationship.[4] But in this direction also the way forward is uncertain.

7. *The reasons for the reticence in using the name*

We have shown that in the last resort it cannot be stated with certainty what *YHWH* means. All attempts at etymological interpretations, which always at the same time of course are seeking to convey the religious content of the word and are influenced by definite theories about this, suffer from its ambiguity. The greatest difficulties in this direction arise from that fence which the biblical tradition has erected around the name of God as a result of the realisation of the

[1] The name Jehu suggests that a *hû'* is not contained in the name Yahweh ; cf. Th. Bauer, op. cit. p. 31.

[2] This must be the view of K. G. Kuhn, who sees Yahweh as a verbal inflexion of a nominal plural. (*Orientalistische Studien*, E. Littmann-Festschrift (1935) pp. 25 ff.)

[3] See the list in Driver, op. cit. p. 13, and also O. Eissfeldt, *Z.A.W.* (1935), pp. 65 ff. who, through *Yᵉhabhyāh* in Jewish-Babylonian names of the seventh century A.D. (= *YHWH*) supports the interpretation of *-jama* as *YHWH*, and at the same time supposes a much longer survival of unrestrained pronouncing of the name Yahweh than hitherto accepted.

[4] Cf. Schleiff, op. cit. p. 699 ; H. Grimme, *Biblische Zeitschrift* 17 (1926), pp. 29 ff.

dangers inherent in the existence of a proper name for God. This arose partly from a feeling of taboo, partly—as we must be careful not to overlook—from a mature insight into the being of God.

(a) To a naïve sensibility a name for god naturally inspires a certain awe, which is to some extent intelligible from the very fact of name-giving, especially in ancient times. The name puts the personality of its bearer into a usable formula, it embraces his being.[1] " As is his name, so is he ", can be said sarcastically of someone and yet also quite seriously (I Sam. xxv. 25). Thus God's being is concentrated in His name. The name is both the quintessence of His person and the bearer of His power, the pronouncing of His name gives a concrete form to all that can be perceived in the god. But not least is there the specifically divine, the holy and awe-inspiring (*pil'î*, Judges xiii. 18), visible and efficacious in it. Thus the name of God is a numinous force, *nikhbādh*, " mighty ", and *nôrā'*, " feared " (Deut. xxviii. 58), as is God Himself.[2]

(b) This, however, is a one-sided approach to the name, in that in the God of Israel it is not only dynamic and fearful qualities that are discernible. True, we must also reckon fully with the fact that the vast majority of the biblical authors, as they wrote down the tetragram in their texts, must have had in their minds a style of speech which made bold to pronounce the name as it was without hesitation. That is true at least of those who began their prayers with the word *YHWH* in the vocative as the most personal expression of trust and hope.[3] They experienced in the name the positive, protecting, element of divine

---

[1] Cf. J. Pedersen, *Israel* (1926), pp. 245 ff.

[2] Because the name is feared its pronunciation is avoided ; Amos vi. 10 (cf. Zeph. i. 7) ; Hab. ii. 20.

[3] Cf. Ps. xxvii. 4 : the presence of Yahweh is ecstasy.

presence and reality, not just the negative element that rejected and endangered men. Correspondingly, we seldom find in the O.T. writers themselves a tendency to diminish the use of the name, except in E. and Ecclesiastes.[1] Even where 'elôhîm is found, there is mention of the " name " as the power of God: " O God, help me through thy name and grant me justice through thy power! " (Ps. liv. 1). It is hard to believe that these authors are under the spell of the numinous awe which certainly dominated the redactors, when, for example, in Lev. xxiv. 11, in a narrative of the cursing of God, they inserted the " name " as the object of the curse,[2] or the Greek translator of Exod. iv. 24 wrote ἄγγελος κυρίου for Yahweh.[3] True, the feeling of distance is a definite feature of the Yahweh-religion from its beginning and even constitutes one of its basic elements (cf. Exod. iii. 6, where Moses fears to look towards God, and especially Isa. viii. 13: " It is He that fills you with fear and terror ").[4] But, as a result of a revival of ancient dynamic modes of heathen thought which came perhaps to Judaism through close contact with ceremonies of swearing allegiance, the feeling of distance was overcome, as may be seen in the Masoretes' treatment of the name of God and the use of shēm by the Samaritans.

(c) But a fundamental and spiritually powerful criticism of the name of God, a determined challenge towards its myth-based construction preceded these narrowly-channelled anxieties and probably involuntarily promoted the growth of their parasitic tendrils. This criticism is to be seen in the procedure of the

[1] Cf. Bousset-Gressmann, op. cit. pp. 307 f.; B. Jacob, Im namen Gottes, pp. 164 ff.

[2] Baudissin, Kurios, vol. ii, pp. 174 ff.

[3] See further Geiger, op. cit. pp. 264 ff.

[4] See also Joshua xxiv. 19 ; Lev. x. 3.

so-called elohistic recension of the Hexateuchal narratives in dealing with the name of God, and then in the confirmation of the development of those thoughts in the so-called elohistic psalter, Ps. xlii to lxxxiii.[1]

Whatever answer we give to the still open question of the literary independence of the elohistic narratives it cannot be denied that in them the first large-scale attempt is made to break with the use of the proper name Yahweh.[2] Yet the tradition that this name had a decisive significance in the foundation of Moses proved a hindrance to this attempt. The result of that tradition is to be seen in the text as it stands in that in those parts of the narrative which follow after the theophany to Moses in Exodus III the name Yahweh is gradually introduced. But the fact that this happens only irregularly leads to the supposition that the use of Yahweh in E is entirely due to the alterations of redactors, whereas the original author always used 'elôhîm.[3]

Whatever reasons he had for this procedure, he at least showed unmistakably that the person of God cannot be distinguished from other individuals by the normal method of using names, since divinity is the possession not of several but only of One.[4]

8. *The divine name in the narrative of Yahweh's revelation to Moses, Exodus, iii. 14*

(a) This well-known holding back by E from the name Yahweh is especially noticeable when he comes

[1] Cf. H. Gunkel, *Einleitung in die Psalmen* (1933), pp. 447 ff.

[2] Baudissin, *Kyrios*, ii, p. 171, disagrees.

[3] See J. Wellhausen, *Die Composition der Hexateuchs*[2] (1889), p. 72.

[4] R. Kittel, op. cit. p. 258, sees in the use of Elohim not a monotheistic tendency but only a pre-Yahweh form linking on to Canaanite terminology. If E really proceeded so much on the correct lines of the *Religionsgeschichtliche Schule*, he must have done it with some educative purpose : what was that?

of necessity to speak of the name, in the story of the revelation of Yahweh to Moses in Exodus iii.[1] That the climax of this narrative was the imparting of this divine name is shown, quite apart from the obviously added verse 15,[2] by the Priestly account of the same event in Exod. vi. 2 f. Nevertheless the key words in Exod. iii. 14 do not contain the tetragram; but to the question what information Moses is to give about the name of God speaking to him, God answers Moses " I am that I am. And he said, Thus shalt thou say to the sons of Israel, ' I am ' has sent me to you." These enigmatic words are either to explain the name Yahweh by an alliterative description of its meaning, or else, in approaching near to the form of the name, expressly to avoid it and allow its use to seem problematical.

(b) It is at first sight tempting to interpret the clause giving God's answer as an ingenious attempt at an interpretation of the meaning of the name Yahweh which is nowhere otherwise discussed; and this is usually what happens. In that case the clause would be analogous to the attempt to explain *hawwāh* from *hayyîm* (Gen. iii. 20) or *Abraham* out of *hāmôn* (Gen. xvii. 5), i.e. as a very free connexion with the given word-picture, as narrators like to do, and thereby guide the attention of their hearers to the symbolic content of the name. The fact that there is no small number of philologically unacceptable etymologies in the Bible stories is a strong argument for supposing that that is also the case here, when we have to reckon with the naïve determination of all those attempts to arrive at the meaning of the names, however different may be the moods in which they are made.[3] In the

[1] To E belong verses 1, 4b, 6, 9-14.

[2] " And God spake *further* to Moses. . . ."

[3] Cf. on Jacob, Gen. xxvii. 36 with xxv. 26, and the satirical play upon the words Edom and Seir in xxv. 25, and the spiteful puns about Moab and Ammon in Gen. xix. 37 f.

present instance the moral would be indubitable: the name of God is intended to express something like existence (*hāyāh*).[1] But how would that be meant? Surely every name, also every divine name, obviously embraces an expression of existence, in that it denotes a concrete phenomenon. And what is the point of the relative clause " that I am "?

To this there is no certain answer, and this circumstance therefore attracts interpreters since Rashi until today to continue discovering hidden meanings in this *'ehyeh*. Thereby can much be said that is correct and unassailable about a conception of existence or reality, and many a speculation about the weaning of faith from magic,[2] about the " Deus revelatus " and " Deus absconditus ", be indulged in. But even so the results are as speculative as the LXX with its ἐγώ εἰμι ὁ ὤν,[3] which certainly has but little to do with *'ehyeh 'asher 'ehyeh*.[4]

(*c*) The speculative hidden meaning of a ὁ ὤν in the Hebrew text is in the last resort impossible to define. The words lose their unfathomability as soon as one refrains from regarding them as aetiological etymology. For the supposition that they are such becomes very questionable, owing to marked formal

[1] Cf. Job iii. 16, *lô' 'ehyeh*, " I do not exist ", Gen. i. 2 (?), ii, 18.

[2] Cf. Buber, op. cit. p. 85. An interpretative periphrasis suggests " I exercise power " (J. Hempel, *Gott und Mensch im A.T.*).

[3] That might conceivably be a translation of *'ehye 'asher yihyeh*; cf. P. Haupt, *Orientalische Literaturzeitung*, xii, pp. 211 ff. W. F. Albright, *Journal of Biblical Literature*, xliii (1924), pp. 370 ff.

[4] For the nota relationis *'asher* is ambiguous. The probability that *'asher 'ehyeh* could fulfil the static function of a participle is slight. For where in Hebrew the participial function of a verb is envisaged in a relative clause, its participial form is entirely usual, cf. *'asher yôshēbh* (Deut. i. 4) or *'asher mebhaqeshîm* (Jer. xxxviii. 16), etc., and a participle corresponding to the speculative Greek ὤν does not exist in Hebrew.

and material gaps which are not explicable by the general strangeness of O.T. etymologies.

Against the etymological interpretation, is (i) the fact that the consonants forming the tetragram are ignored in so far as it is a question of *hāyāh* instead of *HWH*, which might have been expected. But *HYH* and *HWH* sound different to the ear, however closely they may be connected.[1] (ii) The imperfect form *'ehyeh* leaves out the preformative *yôdh* which is decisive in the formation of the tetragram. The necessity of using the first person in a narrative context would have stopped an author desirous of explaining the form *YHWH* from any explanation along these lines. (iii) Nowhere else in the O.T. literature is *HYH* cited as the root of *YHWH*. For it is impossible to interpret every occurrence of the form *'ehyeh* or something like it on God's lips [2] as an echo of Exod. iii. 14. (iv) The " revelation-style " is by far the least suitable form for etymology. " Etymologies are not revealed." [3]

(*d*) In that case the situation is either that the words *'ehyeh 'ªsher 'ehyeh* and *'ehyeh* by itself constitute an incursion into the original text such as was later called a *tiqqûn sôpherîm*,[4] and constitutes nothing other than a refusal to enquire into the name of God, or that the author himself intended this refusal.

(*a*) Under the former alternative, the coming into existence of the phrase would have been something like this; the narrator, setting aside all reflexion of his own, and following the tradition before him, had recounted how God had given His own name as

---

[1] In Isa. xxxviii. 11, *yāh yāh* is vocative of the short form in litany-style repetition.

[2] Cf. e.g. Hos. i. 9 ; Ezek. xiv. 11, xxxiv. 24, etc.

[3] H. Gunkel, *Genesis*[5] (1922), xxii.

[4] For this concept cf. E. Ehrentreu, *Untersuchungen über die Massora* (1925), pp. 8 f.

authentication of what He said.   But this authentication also pointed unmistakably to the polytheistic
background of the whole narrative, namely the in
itself problematical fact [1] that the Israelites could be
in doubt which of the divinites who might conceivably
be regarded as God the Father (cf. Josh. xxiv. 14 f.)
had imposed his charge upon Moses.   It is easy to
comprehend how in these circumstances a so pointed
mythical declaration about the revelation of a divine
name at the most important passage of the tradition of
redemption could be objected to.   It would be felt as
an authentication as Father-gods of the " other gods "
mentioned in Joshua xxiv.   Thus a redactor, at the
same time influenced by elohistic propensities, could
easily have omitted the name from the divine answer
because at this particular juncture, and in the text of
a divine saying, the whole complex of questions connected with the name was felt to be too difficult.[2]   The
violence of the alteration is glossed over in masterly
fashion by turning to account the phrase already present
in verse 12, *'ehyeh 'immākh*—" I am beside thee ".
Almost unnoticeably the *HYH* has been heightened
into an existential function and the mystery of divine
being set forward as the most significant element in all
invocation.   With the context the author of the
tiqqûn is not further concerned.

(β) Less easy than this supposition of an early redac-
tion is the interpretation of the text as a rejection of
the question directed to God on the part of the narrator
himself.   It is in that case given in the form of an
inconsequential tautology " I am I ".   One might
make this conjecture since the divinity striving with

[1] On this cf. A. Alt, op. cit. pp. 12 ff.

[2] A possible analogy is *shîlôh* in Gen. xlix. 10.   There may have
been a name for the Messiah in the text there which for some
reason it seemed advisable to conceal.

Jacob in Jabbok refused him his name (Gen. xxxii. 29): " Why askest thou my name? " The messenger of God who met Samson's parents answered similarly and added the reason that his name was *pil'î* " belonging to God " and therefore unattainable by, or dangerous for, men (Judges xiii. 18). But the supposition that an analogous desire to suppress the name may have influenced the narrator comes up against the difficulty that in the entire picture of the rencontre there is not the very slightest suggestion of a refusal on the part of God. On the contrary, the second part of verse 14—" thou shalt say to the children of Israel, ' *'ehyeh* ' has sent me ", looks like an accession to the request.[1] The refusal would then be expressed only in the word *'ehyeh*, a stylistic difficulty which would be very noticeable in this highly prominent passage, and which is also not present in the two passages which support this thesis. For that reason we may assume that alternative (α) is the more likely.

9. *The name Yahweh as the Foundation of the Old Testament proclamation about God*

The O.T. texts about Yahweh take many forms, and vary in the intensity of their faith and in their forms of expression according to the ability and character of many great and lesser authors; sometimes they are boxed up curiously in strange thoughts, but mostly expressed in clear and ordered terms. The link with history, with the here and now, takes very many forms, but never loses its basic motif—that Yahweh is Lord. Man has no power over him; any influence he may exercise is limited to that allowed to a slave over his lord. But no man can adjure Yahweh to do what he wants, and anyone who tries to has felt

[1] Buber, op. cit. pp. 237 f. ; Grether, op. cit. p. 22.

no breath of His spirit. The texts cohere together
into a consistent picture of God in such a way that its
complete interpretation springs from the apprehension
of the Thou who speaks to man. This power is
experienced not so much as something total, as something whose vitality showed itself in the will directed
to the salvation and consummation of existence—that
is the revelation for whose sake the history of Yahweh
with Israel, its beginning, its zenith and its passing
over into the history of God with the world has been
collected together in the canon of the O.T. Its
content might be summarised by saying that the name
of Yahweh is the basic mould of all O.T. predications
about God, or that the figure of Yahweh is the mould
of biblical revelation.

(a) This judgement, it is true, is immediately confronted by the difficulty that the God who bears the
proper name Yahweh is thereby labelled as one God
among many: indeed important early sources of faith
in God, such as the two-fold traditions of the decalogue
(Exod. xx. 3 ff. and Deut. v. 7 ff.) or Psalms such as
lviii and lxxxii, narratives such as Joshua xxiv. 14 f.,
prophecies like Amos v. 26, confirm that in the worship
of Yahweh there was always a distinction between
Yahweh and the gods which was explicitly understood
as well as implicitly felt. True, that was mostly by
way of rejection of the other gods, but there are also
definite instances of mythical thought. In a strange
land it is impossible to sing Yahweh's songs (Ps.
cxxxvii. 4), it necessitates the service of other gods
(I Sam. xxvi. 19); in Damascus Rimmon is lord
(II Kings v. 18) in Moab Chemosh (Judges xi. 24;
II Kings iii. 27). Foreign soil is impure: Amos vii.
17; Hos. ix. 3 f. But the surest proof of the vitality
of mythical thinking in the congregation of Yahweh is
the fact that the rivalry of the " other gods " did not

6

cease from producing new crises of faith from generation to generation. The narrative in I Kings xviii.
17 ff. shows it in the ordeal staged by Elijah in order
to prove that his God was the right one for the in-
habitants of the Carmel district to worship.[1] Here
too, as almost always, the crisis was resolved as a result
of political development in which the shifting of power
among the gods seems to have found expression. State-
gods of foreign powers, " the whole host of Heaven "
(II Kings xxi. 3) at times found an official place alongside Yahweh;[2] Ishtar, " the Queen of Heaven "
(Jer. vii. 18), Adonis, the Syrian vegetation-Baal (Isa.
i. 29 f.) attracted the women. " According to the
number of thy cities are thy gods " is the verdict of
Jer. ii. 28. Nearly every page of the prophets testi-
fies to opposition to faith in Yahweh and threats to its
unity.

(b) Besides deviations into foreign mythologies there
are also signs of lack of feeling for the numinous
altogether. In quiet times and in secure strata of the
people Yahweh was accepted with a certain official
matter-of-factness which led to reserve in face of
mythical conceptions. The political cleavage of
Yahweh's people led, especially in the Northern
Kingdom, to a receptivity towards alien myths, which
leads one to infer an ominous lack of poise and instinct
in religious questions. " They sacrificed unto the
Baalim, and burned incense to images " (Hos. xi. 2).
They cry unto Yahweh " not with their heart " (Hos.
vii. 14), incapable of stomaching His demands (Jer.

---

[1] A. Alt, *Das Gottes Urteil auf dem Karmel*, Beer-Festschrift
(1955), pp. 1 ff., explains the events as a political *force majeure*
of the State-God of Israel against the Phoenicians.

[2] Ezra viii. 10 ff. probably refers to Egyptian cults. Official
syncretism appears since Solomon. Cf. R. Kittel, op. cit. ii,
pp. 192 ff.

vi. 10). The child-sacrifices of Manasses' and Ahaz'
times are like acts of despair, enheartening people
without roots. On the other hand, we find a vulgar
contentedness of which prophets can only speak in
scorn and disgust. The Holy One of Israel is despised
and spurned (Isa. i. 4) since their wills are not respon-
sive, but they are led on merely by animal impulses
so that the symbolic gods seem a more natural object
of worship. In undisturbed enjoyment of bourgeois
prosperity they are like " wine left on the lees " (Jer.
xlviii. 11), " lying upon the lees " (Zeph. i. 12) unmoved
by the fear of God: " Yahweh does neither good nor
evil "—i.e. his activity is fundamentally doubtful.
" He will not make investigations ", Ps. x. 4; cf. Jer.
v. 12). What is " Yahweh's work "? (Isa. v. 12).
Only scorn accompanies the phrase, " Let Him hasten
with His work that we may yet experience the counsel
of the Holy One of Israel! " (Isa. v. 19).

Thus does the comfortable bourgeois seek to
ridicule the god-inspired speaker and call him mad
(Hos. ix. 7; Jer. xxix. 26); the fear of God is a mere
human tradition learned by rote (Isa. xxix. 13), no
real experience. Even the patriarchal narrators have
not resisted the temptation to introduce a frivolous
feature of this kind into the story of Jacob, who in
his extremity dares to support his lies with Yahweh's
name while cautiously disassociating himself from it.
(" Yahweh, thy God ", Gen. xxvii. 20.)

Such aberrations, it is true, are not solely explained
by mythical thinking, for which " God " means a
changeable and therefore crippled authority. But the
history of religions corroborates the inference that the
indifference of sly self-seeking is wont to be bolstered
up by mythical ideas of God: the power of a God so
limited is also curtailed. It was decisive in Yahwism
that the figure of Yahweh, however belarded with

mythical *traits*, was no special god with a limited sphere, but infused unlimited authority into every sphere of life. " Seek me and ye shall live " (Amos v. 4); so challenge and promise are fused, and the mythical form of speech and thought about Him lose their human values and become the monumental means of expression of a cosmic will.

(c) Thus, Yahweh, in the minds of His proclaimers, is never a mere abstraction, nor an euhemeristic concept, but stands before them and compels them as an audible, visible and felt personality. They do not get the impression of dreaming when His hand lays hold of them, Jeremiah speaks stern words about such an imagined reception of revelation (Jer. xxiii. 28). They see Yahweh and yet are unable to describe Him. The picture seen by the inmost eye has nothing of the naïveté of mythical conception, it is in every respect compulsive and imposing. Especially instructive is the theophany described in Ezekiel. A miraculous picture is sketched, consisting of a complex of animals and wheels and beating wings, and not till later is the attempt made to say what is essential in carefully composed words: there was something there which seemed like an image of the majesty of Yahweh. The prophet almost recoils from the fact that he has previously said that what sat upon the likeness of a throne looked like a man. So he repeats, correcting himself, the whole proclamation, leading it up to *kābhôdh*. *Kābhôdh*, the royal *plērōma*, comes in as substitute for person or man (Ezek. i).[1]

In the light of passages such as this there is no ground for attaching decisive importance to the frequent

[1] The apocalyptist of Dan. vii, speaking of the " Ancient of days " and His white hair, himself shows, albeit unconsciously, that he is using a temporal conception to express authority, when he speaks of God as being old.

human and mythical features in the picture of Yahweh, where our object is to ascertain the essence of faith in Him. It is a mere figure of speech to say that Yahweh has a mouth or a heart, that His lips are full of wrath, or that His arm is stretched out like that of a giant. The necessities of artistic imagination are the prime cause of the use even in religious poetry, of such forms, as seem to be the only possibility for the portrayal of voluntary and masculine *motifs* in religious experience. The astringent originality of personal experience expresses itself in them, regardless of possibilities of interpretation which could lead one astray from the central experience of revelation. The strong resolution of the prophets, just as the hymnodic or pathetic fervour of the poets, is born out of the contact with the personal will of Yahweh. That is the real genesis of the conception of divine grandeur and power which infuses with commanding power each mind that traces the traditional manifestations, so that out of even the humblest and most scanty sources about the cult of Yahweh, the question of its reality arises automatically and no reader is freed from the existential judgement over the divine Person and His will.

(*d*) The great poetical attempts to see the divine action of Yahweh in the dimensions of time (Ps. xc) and space (Ps. cxxxix) projected into infinity also lead us up to the limits of human understanding of personality, but nevertheless do not give up the revealed knowledge of the divine personality and so do not diverge from the lineage of biblical religion. The unusually speculative *traits* of these meditations are neither resigned nor quietistic, but arrive out of the feeling of responsibility of man addressed by God, which threatens to rise to the level of purely numinous awe. If the poet seeks " knowledge " (Ps. cxxxix. 6) concerning the secret of divine existence he comes

up against a " wonder " (*pele'*), and the knowledge
that Yahweh is ever beholding him and enfolding
him gives rise in his mind to a creaturely anxiety:
" Whither shall I go from Thy spirit, whither
flee from Thy countenance? ". The threatening
words of Amos (ix. 2 f.) live in his mind and the desire
to flee from God induces a basic feeling of the " religion
of holiness ",[1] such as the poem of Job has especially
pictured in words of helpless anguish born of the dark
depths of experience. It sounds like a bitter travesty of
Ps. viii. 5 when Job vainly seeks to escape from God:
" let me alone! What then is man, that Thou
dost make him so great and workest Thy will upon
him, inspecting him every morning, testing him every
moment? Wherefore dost Thou not look away from
me for one moment? " (Job. vii. 16 ff.). Then his
feeling of guilt stifles him in a mood of panic: " Whether
blameless or wicked, it matters not—He destroys "
(Job. ix. 22). But Ps. cxxxix. like Ps. lxxiii. 13 ff. is
an example of how so crippling a feeling, of being the
victim of demonic arbitrariness, finds its way back to
the peaceful mood of the hymn to the Lord and
expresses itself in the prayer " lead me in Thy eternal
way! "

(*e*) Naïve mythical thinking is more easily to be
seen in the Priestly texts about man as the " moulded
image " and " similitude " of God (Gen. i. 26, ix. 6).
It is discernible in the " we-style " of God's speech and
is most strongly expressed in the word *ṣelem*. It is
further significant that the attached asyndetic form
kidhᵉmûthēnû " corresponding to our similitude " attempts to turn away the massive realistic expression
in the direction of allegory. But in strict logic, without
any abstraction or spiritualisation, the sentence " We

---

[1] J. Hänel, *Die Religion der Heiligkeit* (1931), i, pp. 317 ff.

will make men as our moulded image, corresponding to our likeness " is saying two things: (1) that the God who speaks has a shape, like all gods, which man can portray as *ṣelem*, and can therefore imagine; and (2) that by looking at man's figure we may arrive at the conclusion " God looks something like that ".[1] That the text must be spiritualised follows not so much from that it goes on to say that God made them as man and woman, for both these are " man ", as from the context of the narrative, of which it can fairly be said that it " demythologises its material as far as possible ".[2]

(*f*) The same observation is justified about the few relatively tangible pieces of evidence about the early phases of the cult of Yahweh. The definitely masculine picture of God which evolved from the tradition beyond the pioneer work of Moses, determined that O.T. piety shall be basically not only obedience and loyalty, but also love, not because the myth was especially imposing, but because in it the unknown power of the Holy was transformed into the purposeful will of the leader-God, binding man to obedience and loyalty. Yahweh " the man of War " (Exod. xv. 3) is no berserk: He fights not for the sake of fighting but for the sake of the victory of His resolve to give this people which bears the name " God fights ", and is bound to Him by oath, its inheritance, the necessities of life, and joy. To understand how much more than

---

[1] That the shape of His body is meant is shown by V, 3. A silver coin of about the fifth century B.C., coming probably from Gaza, with the letters *YHW*, shows a bearded man sitting upon a winged chariot. Reproduction in J. Hempel, *Die althebräische Literatur* (1930), p. 111. Is Yahu here portrayed as territorial God of a heathen province, or heathen god as territorial God of an Israelite province? Cf. H. Gressmann, *Z.A.W.* (New Series), ii (1925), pp. 16 f.

[2] G. von Rad, *Die Priesterschrift im Hexateuch* (1934), p. 168.

theoretical the loyalty between God and people was, their mutual *ḥesedh*, it is of special significance to note how great a part is played by impulsive emotion from this powerful figure of God. In the Decalogue and elsewhere, Yahweh is called a jealous God—*'ēl qannâ'* (Exod. xx. 5, etc.).[1] As this can even be His " name " (Exod. xxxiv. 14) a description of the mystery of His person, the importance of the term for the knowledge of Yahweh is also prominent in the tradition. Its influence upon the whole biblical message must not be overlooked. The precise meaning of the word is that Yahweh wills to be loved by those He loves, that loyalty to Him must be unlimited, because mutual. There is scarcely any stronger expression for the personal, emotion-born relationship of God to man, which is only half-seen if one looks at the negative character of threatening. An inmost sphere of God's life is shyly pointed to when there is talk of an elemental emotion which, as painful reaction against an alien invasion into this sphere, moves with compelling power. As *'ēl qannâ'* Yahweh is no Baal at rest in himself, because love makes itself felt in Him. It is a feature of the virile seriousness of this message from God that its expression is veiled in negation and must be felt. *Qin'āh*, used of men, is wounded love, the raging " gnawing at the bones " (Prov. xiv. 30) correlative of *neqāmāh*, vengeance, the affronted sense of justice and honour. The jealous, avenging God (Nahum i. 2; Ps. xliv. 1) is thus He who can be wounded at heart, is person in the full sense as bearer of sensitivity,[2] to be

---

[1] The thought appears so spontaneously that it stands out sharply from its context in the decalogue's text. It belongs to the old kernel of Yahweh's message. Through its use as a paraenetic threat in Deuteronomy, its already veiled kernel, love, is so clamped down as to be scarcely discernible.

[2] Cf. *Ka'as*, Ps. lxxxv. 5, etc., and the verb *hikh'îs*.

provoked by suspicious doubt as to His serious demands. His advice and actions are steeped in emotion, and so fully and unreservedly that He appears to need that men whom He trusts should act in accordance with His directions. Thus one might say that the *'ēl qannâ'* is a young God, since only an old man such as the dogmatic Eliphaz (Job. v. 2) finds jealousy foolish. The emotional witness of the conception and its logical adequacy become clearer if one attempts to develop its consequences in an ordered manner, as happens with those glosses on the text of the decalogue which attempt to make it support a theory of retaliation.[1] The concept can only be understood within the framework of the general picture of Yahweh, the man who is no man but a God. In other words the imponderable which is dynamic and demonic takes form in the imponderability of the person of the Holy. In face of it, man is only in doubt when he tries to evade it. Then he incurs the wrath.[2] But the feeling yet teaches man that it is better to fall " into the hand of Yahweh " than into the hand of man, " for His mercy is great " (II Sam. xxiv. 14).

(*g*) It is in His guiding that Yahweh is seen and recognised as Lord. It is total, covering the whole of life, as even the classic basic text of the torah, the Decalogue,[3] suggests. The " I " of the speaking God

---

[1] Exod. xx. 5 f. ; Deut. v. 9 f. is theologically naïve, and therefore itself had to submit to a further unhappy correction (" who love me ", " who hate me ").

[2] Wrath is also a periphrasis for the operations of the Holy, which presupposes its being expressed in personal feelings. Wrath is never intended as the essence of God in the O.T., as it is elsewhere (cf. R. Otto, op. cit. p. 123), but it denotes a definite emotional reaction of His. *Paḥadh yiṣḥāq* (Gen. xxxi. 42) is not Yahweh, but a Baal of Beersheba.

[3] To the attempts to trace the origins of the Decalogue back to Moses it has rightly been objected (most recently by L. Köhler,

addresses a " thou ". Who is thus addressed, a community or an individual, remains at first sight obscure. What is clear, however, is the practical pointedness of the address: " I am Yahweh, thy God ", in the phrase " other gods shall not be present for thee in despite of me ". If other gods were present for thee, that would mean not a theoretical recognition of their existence, but practical willing adoption of their powers, " service " in the broadest sense. That sort of thing is not to happen " in despite of me ". Thus this is no informative declaration on the existence or non-existence of gods, as distinct from God: the theological term monotheism has only a subordinate significance when applied to the biblical religion, since it is not practically effective in life. The God who speaks " to thee ", who declares His will authoritatively and intelligibly to human understanding, is God for those who hear Him. That this relationship with authority excludes all others at all similar, that is the clause, felt to be self-evident, which impelled the biblical belief in God inexorably beyond all limits of people and myth. The prohibitive form " thou shalt have none other gods " (to which most of the other clauses of the Decalogue also point) makes clear that the sovereignty of the clause as a way of life is exclusive. The extent of its infusion into the mythical formative impulses of the religions of race, even into the ever-luxuriant growth of myth in religious thought in general, may now be measured by surveys over the field of the history of religion. But the men to whom

Theologische Rundschau, New Series I (1929), pp. 161 ff.) that they can lead to no certainty, nor even to a probable result. The two texts are self-subsistent, which means that they are in any case older than any of the great narrative sources of the Hexateuch, into which they have been inserted at an important juncture, the account of the constitution of the community.

the sentence was originally spoken felt themselves at first merely reminded of the will of their God Yahweh in a way that was binding and saw themselves obliged to adjust themselves to His will. The strongest germ of religious life, the moving contact of the experience of God with the will, has here emerged.

And here we see what God's lordship is. Overcome both in will and feeling, man receives the unconditionally valid guidance which gives his life significance, balance and purpose, and demands an obedience which is not exhausted in an elegiac cult of a feeling of creatureliness, but shows itself in concrete actions, especially towards other men in the fulfilment of an imposed obligation of loyalty. " We act and we hear " (Exod. xxiv. 7) is the answer of those gathered on the mountain of God to the reception of the law. The realisation that the revelation of God's ways is binding upon men, and not at all just theoretically or generally, but always to the most concrete action, for which it gives the simple and great norms—this may be called the greatest legacy of the O.T. to its readers. It was through the moral demands that the divine experience of Yahweh's congregation was first realised to be universally valid. " O man, you have been told what is reasonable and demanded of thee by Yahweh: do justly, love loyalty, go thy way humbly together with thy God " (Mic. vi. 8). The collective term " man " comes to the prophet unreflectingly out of the dynamic of his divine mission, as with Amos his threatening words against Damascus and the other foreign powers (Amos i. 3 ff.) were born from the unconsciously dawning realisation that the peoples cannot do, and leave undone, what they will, but must pay their accounts to the same divine power whose deep tones had resounded in his ear from Sion (Amos i. 2; cf. ix. 12).

10. *The confessing of allegiance to Yahweh in Deuteronomy* vi. 4

The history-of-religions formula " monotheism " can only be properly applied to O.T. religion in so far as it constitutes a theoretical appraisal of its total contribution to religious perception. But a need to speculate is itself alien to the belief in Yahweh.[1] That is also true of the beginning of the so-called *sh^ema'* of Deut. vi. 4, which might be interpreted as a speculative declaration, if the form of the confession and its context did not show that here too the purpose is not to stimulate or justify thought, but, by means of an emotional declaration about God to energise the will of His confessors. The love towards Yahweh expresses itself in order to foster the community's love for him. The fact that so extensive a value, both in worship and theology, has been assigned to the four brief words *Y^ehôwāh 'elôhénû y^ehôwāh 'ehādh* is justification for a special examination of their much disputed meaning.

The style of the phrase, introduced by a paraenetic formula " Hear, O Israel ", customary only in Deut. (v. 1, ix. 1, xx. 3, xxvii. 9) appears for that very reason to be a quotation of an already-existing formulation. It might well be from an hymn, as it shows the pregnant brevity of hymnody, which is not the style of the rest of Deuteronomy. It contains—and here lies the difficulty—either two clauses, or only one. Grammatically it is easier to suppose that these are two substantival clauses. The first, " Yahweh is our God ", is a kind of basic confession by the people of God, monolatrous, like the first clause of the Decalogue. Beside it comes

---

[1] Ecclesiastes is perhaps an exception ; cf. the obscure phrase about the " one shepherd " (xii. 11).

a second, perhaps also from a hymn, but much more didactic and far-reaching: "Yahweh is one ". If one interprets it on the analogy of a completely similar construction such as Gen. xli. 25, *ḥᵃlôm parʿôh eḥādh hû'* (i.e. it is a question of a single dream, not two), then it would mean that Yahweh is a single person, not several. That would be a pedestrian platitude, but one which can only come into being if one stresses *'eḥādh* and thus arrives at a numbering which is pointless.[1] But the surprising and therefore effective part of the mathematical refinement lies unmistakably in the emphatic stressing of the name, which thereby receives the value of a denotation of species. "Yahweh is one " means that in Yahweh is all that He is, in the last resort exhaustively and exclusively present.[2] Thus the second clause is analytic, not synthetic: it would transcendentally connect the meaning of the first with e.g. Isa. xlv. 6, *'ᵃnî YHWH wᵉ'ên-ʿôdh* and should be rewritten, after clauses such as Deut. iv. 35, *YHWH hû' hā'ᵉlôhîm 'ên-ʿôdh milᵉbhaddô*, or Deut. vii. 9, viz. no one is that, which Yahweh is, God.

This interpretation, however, runs into difficulty in the combination of the two clauses: the question why the more far-reaching clause has the narrower beside it can only be answered by envisaging the possible presence of hymnody in the whole sentence. But the supposition that the second clause does not go beyond the first results in the platitude that *YHWH 'eḥādh* is in fact a numbering which does not become any more

---

[1] The author of Zech. xiv. 9 has obviously interpreted it so. To that corresponds the questionability of his empty sentence, with which he intends to say something quite different from what he actually says.

[2] There is a similar inflexion in e.g. Job xii. 2, *'attem ʿām:* " you are the species man exclusively ".

tolerable if one sees in it a polemic against a
" poly-Yahwism " which attempted to introduce into
Yahwism the many-sidedness of Baal.[1]

No very definite meaning, however, results from
seeing the words hitherto construed as two clauses as
one. In that case 'elôhênû would be in apposition to
YHWH, after which the subject YHWH would be
taken up again: " Yahweh, our God, Yahweh is one ".[2]
This analysis, however bad the style, is more satisfactory than the other, which puts YHWH 'eḥādh in
apposition to 'elôhênû. The feeling that a numeral
does not consort with a proper name must then
prompt periphrastic inflexions such as " Yahweh is our
God, Yahweh as the one and only ". Thereby the
highlight of the monolatry is preserved at the expense
of verbal clarity.

Thus our result is that it is not possible to determine
the meaning of these words in unassailable logical
clarity. This fact, together with the rhythmical force
of the passage and the unmistakable grandeur of the
theme, makes the phrase an unique testimony to the
power of the trust in Yahweh, maintained and yet
restlessly pressing. It seems to stand at a water-shed.
The energising power of the national cult makes use
of an expression that is by now inadequate, and so the
questing depths of perception probe the secret of the
real content of the Yahweh-revelation. Yahweh,

[1] There have indeed been instances of that (cf. Gen. xvi. 13,
xii. 7, xviii. 1 ff., xxviii, and the divine triad in the temple of
Yeb) but there can be no doubt that it is not in place here, and
so doctrinaire a conception could not possibly have arisen in the
brevity of two words.

[2] So the LXX: κύριος ὁ θεὸς ἡμῶν κύριος εἶς ἐστιν. Upon the
early Christian formula εἶς θεός there was probably no influence
from Deut. vi. 4, unless some Greek form of the shema' (I Cor.
viii. 4 ff. (?) ; Jas. ii. 19) deriving from the LXX, supplied that
text ; cf. E. Peterson, Εἶς θεός (1926), pp. 293 ff.

as the epitome of all religious experience, is, according to this confession, the source of one single and
consistent historical revelation.   How many, and
how similar, revelations there may be remains, of
course, a question.   But what has been learned should
be heard.

IV. " LORD " IN LATE JUDAISM

1. *The choice of the word Κύριος in the LXX*

AT this juncture we must discuss the reason for the
choice of the word κύριος in the LXX. Baudissin [1]
has established that the meaning of the O.T. '*ādhôn* is
" being superior to ", in contrast to the exercising of
power over a thing or person. This " being superior
to " could result in the exercise of power over, but is to
be distinguished from it. '*ādhôn* is applied to God in
the O.T. so as to signify that He is the superior being
who " belongs " in this capacity to the speaker
(Baudissin, ii, p. 244). The meaning of κύριος in the
LXX is similar. But Baudissin's argumentation is
not convincing at this point. When he mentions in
support of it that in the O.T. the address '*adhônî* is also
used by the independent person who wishes merely to
convince the person addressed by using this term that
he honours him and wishes to enter into relationship
with him (Baudissin, ii, p. 246), he forgets that such a
mode of address in this context involves the self-
designation of the speaker as " servant " and expresses
the dependence—even when not meant to be taken
literally—of the speaker upon the person addressed: it
is expressive of subjection. The fact that *gᵉbhîrāh*, used
of the queen, is not translated κυρία, as elsewhere,
but by expressions which definitely indicate rule
(Baudissin, ii, p. 253), does not depend upon the fact
that κυρία is only an expression of superiority and not
of rule over someone, but upon the fact that κυρία is
not specially appropriate to the queen: in most of the
passages here cited by Baudissin (loc. cit., n. 1) κυρία

[1] Op. cit. ii, pp. 241-57.

would not convey the meaning sufficiently clearly, since the queen is also κυρία in relation to her slaves.

It is much better to start from the Greek meaning of the word κύριος in the time of the LXX. Since κύριος was not as yet used as an epithet for God in paganism, the ethnic use of it depicted by Baudissin is not relevant for the LXX. Κύριος then, where the specifically hellenistic use of it had made headway, meant " he who can legally dispose ". The element of legality must be stressed all the more because of the uniform substitution of κύριος for the tetragram in the whole LXX, so that it goes back to the first beginnings of this translation. With the choice of κύριος rather than δεσπότης (which was also possible and was even more ready to hand in the Greek of those days) the LXX strongly and consciously affirms that the lord-ship of God is legitimate. Now this affirmation can be based on the historical fact of the election of Israel: He who has saved her from the " smelting-furnace of Egypt " has thereby a legitimate claim upon His people. But the affirmation can also be based on God's creatorship: He who created the universe and mankind is the legitimate Lord. Baudissin supports the former of these alternatives: a main argument for this, apart from that already mentioned, is that κύριος occasionally translates 'elôhîm with the suffix (Baudissin, i, pp. 449 ff.). But here our comprehen-sion of the motives for occasional divergences from the Hebrew text, like these, must always be very uncertain. It must also remain a question whether the LXX, in choosing a translation for ΥHWH (if it is not the case, as Baudissin has meticulously tried to show, that the LXX was influenced by 'adhônāi as a substitute for ΥHWH) confined itself to a term which simply denotes the superior, who gives himself over to those who honour him. Above all, the meaning of the LXX's

7

κύριος which Baudissin assigns to it, from the Greek word and also from its use in the LXX, is most certainly not to be accepted without question, especially as the support of a definite pagan use of it was lacking. Indeed, such a linkage with pagan usage would rather have been a reason for the LXX to avoid its use. The permanent use of κύριος by itself directs our thoughts to the legitimate, unbounded and also invisible power of God to dispose—his ἐξουσία. Even if the motive of the LXX in choosing κύριος has not been correctly hit upon in the foregoing lines, if, for example, it were true that 'ªdhônāi was the pattern for κύριος in the LXX, even so there remains the fact of the far-reach-ingness of this consistently chosen " translation ". The sole word κύριος, without the addition of a divine name (as later on in ethnic use and before in Babylon and Egypt), the appropriate word, was in itself suf-ficient to denote one God—but that means *the one God.* That was bound to suggest to the hearer God's boundless power to dispose over all things. " In the one case (in the ethnic use) the title is added to the name, and the name distinguishes its bearer from numerous other gods and men, who may bear, or may have borne, the title. . . . In the other case (in the LXX) the title is substituted for the name, and the implication is that the bearer is ' sovereign ' in the absolute sense. There is no exact parallel to this in earlier or contem-porary Greek." [1]

2. *" Lord " in the Pseudepigrapha*

Baudissin has produced many arguments against the widely held opinion that 'ªdhônāi as a substitute for the tetragram is older than the LXX. He dates the origin of this artificial form as late as the first century B.C. or A.D. Indeed the use of the tetragram outside

[1] C. H. Dodd, *The Bible and the Greeks*, p. 11.

scripture is perhaps not altogether avoided as late as
the first century A.D., especially because of the vocative
used in the prayer in *IV Esdras*, " dominator domine "
(Baudissin, ii, pp. 189 ff.). The facts are these: A
and Σ have kept the tetragram, written in Hebrew
letters in their Greek translation: for the masoretic
'ᵃdhônāi in the vocative, A once, and Σ often, has
δέσποτα, otherwise κύριος, which Θ gives for *YHWH*
and 'ᵃdhônāi. The masoretic 'ᵃdhônāi *YHWH* is
variously rendered by these translations (Baudissin, ii,
pp. 98 ff.). The Apocrypha use κύριος more or less
frequently up to the time of I, III and IV Maccabees,
so also the *Psalms of Solomon*, in which κύριος or (more
seldom) ὁ κύριος and κύριε are more or less equally
balanced by θεός or ὁ θεός (more frequent) and
also ὁ θεός used as the vocative. In the somewhat later
Assumption of Moses " dominus " is much more prevalent than " deus ", as is also the case, to a lesser
extent, in the *Testaments of the XII Patriarchs*, whereas
IV Esdras, has " altissimus " as its regular denotation
for God, occasionally also " fortis ", once " excelsus ".
In it " dominus " is only found in the vocative for God
and (occasionally with " deus ") in contrast with
angels. The *Syriac Baruch* has mostly " the Almighty "
but " the highest " is also frequent. " Lord " occurs
8 times, " the exalted Lord " once, " God " (or " the
almighty God " 6 times, " the exalted " once. In the
vocative, however, we only once find " Almighty ", 7
times " O Lord, my God ", as many times " Lord ",
and twice " my Lord ". A variegated picture greets
us in *I Enoch*. In the oldest section, *The Vision of
Beasts* (chapters lxxxiii-xc), the Lord of the Sheep in
the parable is a designation for God, but occasionally
we find simply " Lord " (lxxxiii. 2, lxxxix. 14, 15, 16,
18, 54, xc, 17, 21, 34; in the vocative, " My Lord ",
lxxxiv. 6, once " God " (lxxxiv. 1). In the *Similitudes*

the regular designation for God is "Lord of the
Spirits ", more seldom simply " Lord ", " Our Lord ",
" Lord of the World ", " Lord of Kings ", " the
highest ",[1] still less frequently " God " (lv. 3, lxi 10,
lxvii. 1). In the other sections of this collection of
writings we find equally often " God " and " Lord ",
also various periphrases, especially " the highest "
(11 times), " the great one ", " the holy " and " Lord "
with various genitives: " Lord of Heaven ", " of the
world ", " of Creation ", " of glory ", " of judgment ,"
" of righteousness "; also " the God of glory ", the
" King of the World ", " the King of Glory ". In
Jubilees, finally, simply " God " is remarkably predominant (besides composite phrases such as " the
highest God " " the God of Abraham " " our God ",
etc.). The simple " Lord " is almost only found in
the vocative, but we find " Lord " in composite phrases
such as " God the Lord " " the Lord our God " (the
last in the mouth of the angel of revelation), etc. The
Zadokite Fragment [German *Damaskusschrift*] has usually
'ēl, once *'elyôn*, three times *hayyāḥîdh*. In quotations
from the O.T. it usually leaves out *YHWH* or replaces
it by *'ēl*. Forbidden are the oath with Āleph and
Dāleth (*'ªdhônāi*) and with Āleph and Lāmedh
(*'ªlôhîm*) xv. 1 (Schechter).

This evidence admits of another explanation from
that which Baudissin gives, namely that the pseude-
pigraphists wanted their writings to be regarded as
sacred and therefore wrote the tetragram as found in
the O.T. but pronounced it *'ªdhônāi* as they read the
O.T. This would agree with the supposition that the
LXX with its κύριος inclined to the already common

---

[1] " Lord " xxxix. 9, 13, xli. 2, lxii. 1, lxv. 6, lxvii. 3, 10, lxviii. 4 :
" Our Lord ", lxiii. 8 : " Lord of the World ", lviii. 4, " Lord of
Kings ", lxiii. 4, " Lord of Glory ", xl. 3, lxiii. 2 ; " the highest ",
xlvi. 7, lx. 1, lxii. 7.

substitution of *'ªdhônāi* for the tetragram. The considerations which prompted the precise choice of
κύριος remain untouched by this, and precise certainty as to the dating of *'ªdhônāi* is hard to attain,
especially as the use of " Lord " in the *Pseudepigrapha*
reveals noticeable individual divergences. On the
other hand, the copious use of many substitute words
for the designation of God in, e.g. the *Ethiopian Enoch*
reveals a strong anxiety *vis-à-vis* simple terms for
God. In any case Josephus [1] and the sources of the
gospels show that *YHWH* and *'ªdhônāi* had vanished
from everyday speech. The substitute-words in the
Pseudepigrapha give us a good picture of the important
features of the picture of God in writers. In circles
close to Hellenism, from which the authors of the
Letter to Aristeas, of *III* and *IV Maccabees*, and the
Sibylline Oracles [2] spring, κύριος is absent, not from
religious awe, but because it was unintelligible for
Hellenism without the addition of divine names. Philo
was confronted by the fact that in his bible, the LXX,
θεός and κύριος stood side by side as the two chief
designations for God. He saw allegorically in κύριος
a pointer to the βασιλικὴ δύναμις, in θεός one to
the χαριστικὴ δύναμις.[3]

---

[1] Josephus often uses the adjective κύριος : *Contra Apionem*, I,
19 and 146, II, 177, 200 ; he calls the Romans οἱ κύριοι νῦν
'Ρωμαῖοι τῆς οἰκουμένης, *Contra Ap.* II, 41; he also knows that
κύριος corresponds to the Hebrew *'ādhôn*, *Ant.* V, 121. He
entirely avoids using it of God except in one prayer ; *Ant.* XX, 90
(δέσποτα κύριε . . . τῶν πάντων δὲ δικαίως μόνον καὶ
πρῶτον ἥγημαι κύριον) and one quotation from scripture
(*Ant.* XIII, 68). But δεσπότης is common, and δέσποτα in
prayer-invocations to God. See A. Schlatter, *Wie sprach Josephus
von Gott, Beiträge zur Forderung Christliche Theologie*, xiv, 1 (1910),
pp. 8-11 ; and his *Theologie des Judentums*, pp. 25 f.

[2] The same is true of hellenistic-jewish writers such as Artapanus.

[3] *De Somniis*, I, 163. Further passages in Foerster, op. cit.
p. 119, n. 3 ; and see the next note, *infra*.

3. " *Lord* " *in Rabbinic Judaism*

In Palestine in the time of Jesus the literal pronunciation of the tetragram was an unusual occurrence. The Rabbis also linked speculations on to the two chief names for God in their bible, *YHWH* and *'elôhîm*, and these concerned the two " measures " of God, the measure of pity and the measure of judging, but they assigned them to the names differently from Philo.[1]

In general speech *'ādhôn* has largely disappeared. True, it is still occasionally used as a mode of address together with a title, *'adhônî hārôphē'*;[2] to the king, *'adhônî hammelekh*;[3] to the high-priest, *'adhônî kôhēn gādhôl*;[4] *'adhônênû werabbênû* to the king.[5] Of Pharoah it is said that he has called himself *'adhôn hā'ôlām*.[6] Of God *'ādhôn* is still used in various ways, together with *hā'ôlam, kol hā'ôlāmîm, lekhol ma'asîm, lekhol bâ'ê 'ôlām, kol beriyyôth*.[7] When the Rabbis discussed the problem who was the first to call God *'ādhôn*, we see the significance which they attached to this name.[8] This makes clear the connexion between being " Lord " and " Creator ". In general the Rabbis use for " Lord " *rabh, rabbā', rabbôn, rabbônā', mârē'*, later also *qîrîs* (κύριος) or *qîrî* (κύριε). *Mârē'* is " Lord " in the most varied uses of this word: master of a slave, owner of property, lord of the soul, i.e. of passions

---

[1] On this see A. Marmorstein, " Philo and the names of God " in the *Jewish Quarterly Review* (New Series), xxii, pp. 295-306, and the literature there cited.

[2] *Jer. Berakoth* 9b, Dalman, *Worte Jesu*, p. 349.

[3] Dalman, loc. cit.

[4] *Leviticus Rabba* iii, 5 on ii, 1; Dalman, loc. cit.

[5] Ibid.

[6] *Exod. Rabba* v, 14 on v, 2; Marmorstein, op. cit. p. 63.

[7] Instances in Marmorstein, pp. 62 f.

[8] First Simeon ben Jochai (*c.* A.D. 150) *Bab. Berakoth* 7b; Marmorstein, p. 62.

(corresponding to κύριος), as a mode of address (always with a personal pronoun) it is a courteous address from inferiors (servants and subjects) and also between equals, corresponding to 'ādhôn in the O.T.[1] Of God, mārē' is used together with sh*emayyā'[2] and 'âlmā',[3] marî as a mode of address to God is found, e.g. *Gen. rabba* 13, 2, on ii. 5, the abstract mârûthā' d*e* 'âlmā' occurs *Gen. rabba* 55, on xxii. 2.[4] *Rabh* is in general, even without suffix, the teacher,[5] but especially used in the suffix form rabbî as a mode of address to a teacher. The suffix soon lost its meaning.[6] But rabh also means lord in other respects, e.g. of the slave.[7] *Rabbî* is in any case a form of address showing unusual respect.[8] Besides rabh we find rabbôn (later ribbôn) which in the gospels is used as a mode of address and is also found in the Targums[9] for the biblical 'ādhôn where it does not refer to God. But later this word is practically used only for God, especially in the phrases rabbôn shel 'ôlām, rabbôn hâ'ôlāmîm.[10]

Another important word is ba'al, which denotes ownership[11] and in parables often means God, in the phrase ba'al habbayith.[12] Some further names of God compounded with ba'al must also be mentioned[13]—albeit

[1] Dalman, op. cit. p. 267, where texts are cited.

[2] *Qoheleth Rabba* on iii. 2.

[3] *Genesis Rabba* 99, on xlix. 27 : Marmorstein, p. 94, n. 46.

[4] Marmorstein, p. 93, n. 44.

[5] *Pirqe Aboth* I, 6, 16. On rabbi cf. also C. H. Moore, *Judaism* iii, pp. 15-17.

[6] Dalman, op. cit. p. 274.

[7] *Bab. Taanit* 25b ad fin.; *Bab. Gittin* 23b.

[8] Dalman, op. cit. p. 275.

[9] Dalman, op. cit. pp. 266 f.; Str.-B. ii, p. 25, on Mark x. 51.

[10] Texts in Str.-B. iii, pp. 671 f.; Marmorstein, loc. cit. pp. 98 f.

[11] *Ba'al hatt*e*'ênāh* (= Aramaic mârē' dit'ênta') *Jer. Talmud Berakoth* 5c, line 16.

[12] Marmorstein, pp. 77 f.

[13] Marmorstein, pp. 78 ff.

only " names " in a metaphorical sense. *ba'al dîn* (accuser), *ba'al ḥôbh* (creditor), *ba'al mᵉlā'khāh* (slave-owner), *ba'al hammishpāṭ* (judge), *ba'al happiqqādhôn* (him to whom a pledge is entrusted, in connexion with good deeds); also *ba'al hannehāmôth* and *ba'al hāraḥᵃmîm* and *ba'al hā'ôlām*.

In contrast to Greek usage, in Hebrew and Aramaic " lord " is never used absolutely without an attached noun [1] or suffix, and the address " O lord " is occasionally duplicated.[2]

The lordship of God is important for late Judaism in two connexions—one that God is Lord and Leader of the universe and its history, the other that He is Lord and Judge of the individual. Out of the number of designations for God which name Him in this two-fold insight proceeds the significance of the two spheres of thought. The former is especially (but certainly not exclusively) expressed in the *Pseudepigrapha*, which of course wish to indicate the certainty that the history of the universe, despite all opposing powers, has nevertheless its God-given goal.[3] Characteristic phrases in this connexion are *I Enoch*, ix. 4: σὺ εἶ κύριος τῶν κυρίων καὶ ὁ θεὸς τῶν θεῶν καὶ βασιλεὺς τῶν αἰώνων, and xxv. 3: ὁ μέγας κύριος ὁ ἅγιος τῆς δόξης, ὁ βασιλεὺς τοῦ αἰῶνος; cf. also xxv. 7, xxvii. 3, xci. 13. The predilection of *IV Esdras* and the *Syriac Baruch* for the names " the highest ", " the almighty " also links up with this. For the latter we are referred to the God-names compounded with *ba'al*

---

[1] Dalman, op. cit. p. 268. But there are exceptions—*Bab. Berakoth* 61b, *ad init.*

[2] King Josophat is supposed to have greeted every scholar with *'abhî 'abhî rabbî rabbî marî marî*: *Bab. Talmud, Makkoth* 24a; Dalman, op. cit. p. 268, *ad init.*

[3] How strongly the tension was felt is clear, e.g. from *I Enoch*, lxxxix. 57 f., lxx-lxxi, lxxv-lxxvii, xc. 3.

mentioned above, and should compare also *I Enoch*, lxxxiii. 11, " Lord of judgment ". The Lordship of God is absolute, but yet hidden. Every man can " do deeds of guilt " [1] and be remiss before the " Lord of the work " (*Pirqe Aboth* ii. 19), the kings of the earth can exercise their power against God and His people— that is a result of the sin of the people. If it were to keep a single Sabbath, it would be immediately re- deemed (*Jer. Taanit* 64*a*, ll. 31 f.). This determines the tenor of Judaism towards the powers of this world.

The reason why God is absolute Lord of this world and its course, and over the individual, is because He is " creator of all ": *I Enoch* lxxxiv. 2 f. " Praised art thou, O Lord, King, great and mighty is thy greatness, Lord of the whole creation of the Heaven, King of Kings and God of the entire world! Thy power, sovereignty and greatness endure for eternity and thy Lordship for all generations: all heavens are thy throne for ever and the whole earth the footstool of thy feet. For thou hast created all things and dost rule them." [2] This connexion with the thought of creation gives the lordship of God its final unshakable foundation, gives the ethical obligation its inevitability. *IV Esdras* viii. 60: " the creatures have dishonoured the name of Him who created them, and shown in- gratitude to Him who gave them life. Therefore my judgment is now imminent upon them." *Jer. Talmud, Berakoth* 7 d, l. 61,[3] *berā'thānû la'ašôth resônekhā*. The election of Israel now ranks as far less important than these ideas, and is itself found essentially in the form that God is the Creator of Israel (*Apocalypse of Baruch*, lxxviii. 3, lxxix. 2, lxxxii. 2).

---

[1] Cf. the saying of Rabbi Akiba, *Pirqe Aboth* iii. 16.

[2] Cf. loc. cit. ix 4 f.

[3] Str.-B. iv, pp. 478 ff.

V. *KURIOS* IN THE NEW TESTAMENT

1. *The Secular usage*

In the New Testament, *kurios* denotes the Lord and owner of a vineyard (Mark xii. 9, par.), of an ass (Luke xix. 33), of a dog, (Matt. xv. 27); the master of the (free) steward (Luke xvi. 3, 5, and (?) 8) and the master of unfree slaves (often in the parables, also Acts xvi. 16, 19; Eph. vi. 5, 9; Col. iii. 22, iv. 1); also the person who controls and has to give the word—over the harvest (Matt. ix. 38, par.),[1] or the Sabbath (Mark ii. 28, par.). In oriental courtesy (regarding merely the verbal usage) Elizabeth can call Mary the " mother of my Lord " (Luke i. 43). The subservience of one who sets store by expressing it is expressed in *kurios*, as I Peter iii. 6 points out that Sarah calls Abraham *kurios* (a play upon the words in the LXX of Gen. xviii. 12) and in the quotation of Ps. cx in Mark xii. 36 f. par., and Acts ii. 34. Festus speaks of Nero as the *kurios* (Acts xxv. 26, cf. p. 29, n. 1 *supra*). Κύριος occurs in a stricter sense, implying legal but not actual ownership, inclining towards the adjective κύριος, in Gal. iv. 1: ἐφ᾽ ὅσον χρόνον ὁ κληρονόμος νήπιός ἐστιν, οὐδὲν διαφέρει δούλου κύριος πάντων ὤν. With few exceptions (Matt. xviii. 25, xxiv. 45; Luke xii. 37, 42, xiv. 23, cf. John xiii. 13 f.), this *kurios* is always followed by a genitive in the gospels and Acts, whether it be of a substantive or personal pronoun (also of objects, Luke xx. 13, 15)—a sign of the influence of Palestine usage, cf. *supra*, p. 90, n. 1). But a corresponding genitive is not found in the Epistles—Eph. vi. 5, 9; Col. iii. 22, iv. 1; I Peter iii. 6, also Acts xxv. 26. On Palestine soil

[1] Cf. A. Schlatter, *Mathäusevangelium* (1929), on ix. 38.

this *kurios* may translate *rabbôn, rabh* or *mârē'* (cf. *supra*, p. 88, *ad fin.*). *Kurie* is used often as a mode of address, not only when slaves are addressing their master (they use it exclusively in the gospels) but also by the vine-dresser to the owner of the vineyard (Luke xiii. 8), by the Jews to Pilate (Matt. xxvii. 63), by the son to his father (Matt. xxi. 29—a special case),[1] by Mary to the unknown gardener (John xx, 15), by the jailer at Philippi expressing his awe of his prisoners by calling them *kurioi* (Acts xvi. 30). *Kurie* is also used in addressing angels (Acts x. 4, Rev. vii, 14 (with μου) and the unknown apparition (Acts ix. 5, xxii. 8, 10, xxvi. 15, x. 14, xi. 8). A double *kurie, kurie* (Matt. vii. 21, 22, xxv. 11; Luke vi. 46) also corresponds to Palestinian usage (cf. *supra*, p. 90, n. 2). *Kurie* in the gospels corresponds to *mârî* with suffix, since in speaking of Jesus the evangelists have rendered *rabbî* differently and it was not commonly used in addressing one who was not learned. For *kurie* used in addressing Jesus, *vide infra*, p. 106, *ad fin.*). This *kurie* is never joined to a personal pronoun, nor are the vocatives *epistata* and *didaskale* (except John xx. 28 and Rev. vii. 14) although the vocative " lord " in Palestinian speech always had a suffix attached to it. The vocative " lord " was accorded to a greater number of persons than the designation " lord " and was therefore earlier outmoded. The use of the nominative with the article instead of the vocative (John xx. 28; Rev. iv. 11)[2] is semitic.

Of the genitive-constructions *kurios tēs doxēs* (I Cor.

---

[1] The other son uses no appellation. This sharpens the difference between the words and the deeds of the son who said yes, in that such an appellation upon the lips of a son to his father stresses his subordination. Cf. p. 10, *supra, ad fin.*

[2] Cf. F. Blass, *Grammatik des neutestamentischen Griechisch*, 5th edn., ed. A. Debrunner, § 147, 3.

ii. 8), *tēs eirēnēs* (II Thess. iii. 16a), the latter is supported by *ba'al hannehāmôth* (p. 90, line 5) while the former must be a semitic genitive in the place of an adjective.

Despotēs in the gospels is used in the vocative only in addressing God. It is used of the slave-owner I Tim. vi. 1 f.; Titus ii. 9; I Peter ii. 18; of the Lord and owner of a house II Tim. ii. 21. It is presumably a sign of more precisely chosen language (*vide supra*, p. 9).

2. *God the Lord*

(*Ho*) *kurios* is the name for God in quotations and reminiscences of the O.T., in which the LXX is generally followed: thus Mark i. 3, par., xii. 11, par., xii. 36, par., and Acts ii. 34 (in these cases the LXX has *ho kurios*, but in the N.T. passages the article has been omitted by B, with the support of some other manuscripts), Matt. xxvii. 10; Luke i. 46, and iv. 18, 19; Mark xi. 9, par., John xii. 38(twice); Acts ii. 20, 21, 25, iv. 26, xiii. 10 (most manuscripts omit the article, in contrast to the LXX), xv. 17 (in the LXX *ton kurion* is the reading of A alone, other manuscrips omit it completely), Rom. iv. 8, ix. 28 (the LXX, except for B, has *ho theos* instead of *kurios*), xi. 3 (*kurie* is added to the LXX text), xi. 34 (= I Cor. ii. 16) Rom. xv. 11; I Cor. i. 31 (the words *en kuriōi* are not in that form in the LXX), iii. 20, x. 22 (*ton kurion* is not in the O.T. original), x. 26, II Cor. iii. 16, viii. 21, x. 17; II Thess. i. 9, II Tim. ii. 19 (the LXX has *ho theos* instead of *kurios*), Heb. i. 10, vii. 21, viii. 2 (the LXX omits the article in the Hebrew), viii. 8-10, 11, x. 30, xii. 5-6, xiii. 6; Jas. v. 11, (B omits the article), I Peter i. 25 (LXX *tou theou*), ii. 3, iii. 12 (twice), Jude 9. *Kurios Sabaōth:* Rom. ix. 29; Jas. v. 4. *Kurios ho theos*, followed by a genitive: Matt. iv.

7, 10, par.; Mark xii. 29, 30, par.; Acts iii. 22 (omitting the LXX's personal pronoun), ii. 39 (adding *ho theos hēmōn* to the LXX). *Ho kurios* (LXX adds *pāsēs*) *tēs gēs*, Rev. xi. 4.

In the Markan and Q sources of the synoptics, God is not called (*ho*) *kurios*, except Mark v. 19 (peculiar to Mark), when Jesus says to the healed (pagan) Gergesene demoniac *apangeilon autois hosa ho kurios soi pepoiēken*, and Mark xiii. 20: *ei mē ekolobōsen kurios tas hēmeras* (Matthew and Luke have changed it, or have a different text). In the Gospels *kurios* is used of God in Matthew and Luke's prologues and Matthew's epilogue,[1] also in Luke v. 17, xx. 37—both peculiar to Luke. This shows that '*adhônāi* was not common in the original Palestine community.[2] The marked incidence of *kurios* in the Lukan birth-stories is bound up with the conscious biblical style, and betokens a link with the LXX rather than with contemporary Palestinian usage. Correspondingly, no essential distinction can be made between *kurios* with, and without, the article. Influence of the LXX is seen in the case of *kurios* in certain fixed conjunctions: *cheir kuriou* (Luke i. 66; Acts xi. 21, xiii. 11); *angelos kuriou* (Matt. i. 20, 24; ii. 13, 19, xxviii. 2, Luke i, 11, ii. 9. Acts v. 19; viii. 26, xii. 7 and 23); *onoma kuriou* (Jas. v. 10 and 14); *pneuma kuriou* (Acts v. 9, viii. 39), and the inflexion *legei kurios*, which is added as a formula in Rom. xii. 19; II Cor. vi. 17, and Rev. i. 8; and in Heb. viii. 8, 9, 10, has displaced the LXX's *phēsin kurios*. In these cases *kurios* is always without the article, but it is always with it in the case of *ho logos*

---

[1] Matt. i. 20, 22, 24, ii. 13, 15, 19, xxviii. 2 ; Luke i. 6, 9, 11, 15, 17, 25, 28, 38, 45, 58, 66 ; ii. 9, 15, 22, 23, 24, 26, 39.

[2] I therefore see no reason for Schlatter's contention (*Johannesev.* p. 42) that for Palestinians *kurios* without the article is '*adhônāi*, with it is *mârâ*', i.e. Jesus.

tou kuriou: Acts viii. 25, xii. 24, xiii. 48-9, xv. 35-6, xix. 10 and 20.[1] *Kurios* is also certainly used for God in I Cor. x. 9; I Tim. vi. 15 (with *tōn kurieuontōn*); II Tim. i. 18; Heb. vii. 21, viii. 2; Jas. i. 7, iii. 9 (with *ho patēr*), v. 11a, II Pet. iii. 8; Jude 5 and in Revelation, which in its grandiose style often makes use of the O.T. phrase *kurios ho theos* (plus *pantokratōr*) —i. 8, iv. 8, xi. 17, xvi. 7, xviii. 8, xix. 6, xxi. 22, xxii. 5. Unparalleled formulae occur in Rev. iv. 11—*ho kurios kai ho theos hēmōn*—and xi. 15 (*tou kuriou hēmōn*) and xxii. 6 (*ho kurios ho theos tōn pneumatōn*).

Thus (*ho*) *kurios* is not, especially on Palestinian soil, but also in the community which used the LXX as its bible, a designation for God much used apart from its origin in the Bible. And yet the content inherent in the word *kurios* can be actualised in all its richness at any moment. This is the case in some significant passages. First and foremost, Matt. xi. 25 (almost word for word the same as Luke x. 21): ἐξομολογοῦμαί σοι, πάτερ, κύριε τοῦ οὐρανοῦ καὶ τῆς γῆς, ὅτι ἔκρυψας ταῦτα ἀπὸ σοφῶν καὶ συνετῶν, καὶ ἀπεκάλυψας αὐτὰ νηπίοις. ναί, ὁ πατήρ, ὅτι οὕτως εὐδοκία ἐγένετο ἔμπροσθέν σου· here, the solemn mode of address is a vital component of the willing submission before the sovereignty of the divine *eudokia* and gives it an universal significance. The completely uncaused essence of the divine will is reverently assigned to the Lord over Heaven and earth. The voluntary assent to this good will shows that subservience to this Lord does not produce lack of will-power. A similar line of thought stands behind the parabolic expression *kurios tou therismou* (Matt. ix. 38,

---

[1] *Ho logos tou theou* in Acts is presumably equivalent to *ho logos tou kuriou*. Whether St. Paul in I Thess. i. 8, II Thess. iii. 1, also thought of *ho logos tou kuriou* as the word of God is perhaps not ascertainable and anyhow irrevelant. The point at issue is the influence of the LXX.

par.). The harvest is the great harvest of mankind, its Lord is thus Lord over the whole of world history. In connexion with the day whose dawning is known to no one, not even the Son, St. Paul speaks of God as *ho makarios kai monos dunastēs, ho basileũs tōn basileuontōn kai kurios tōn kurieuontōn*, thus declaring Him to be the director who is sovereign over all the powers which make history upon earth. In a significant passage in Acts, the speech before the Areopagus, St. Luke records St. Paul as seizing upon the word *kurios*, with the genitives *ouranou kai gēs*, to obtain roots for this lordship of God from pagan worship. In this context the lordship of God is traced back to His creatorship. The great part played in Revelation by the full phrase *kurios ho theos ho pantokratōr* is of course no mere accident, but no less important is the newly coined inflexion *ho kurios kai ho theos hēmōn* with which, in iv. 11, the twenty-four elders, who are surely to be thought of as not unconnected with all mankind, as God's creation, describe their relationship with God. In devotional invocations, too, *kurie* can be invested with a special tone, as e.g. Acts i. 24, *su kurie kardiognōsta pantōn*. Jas. iii. 9 must also be mentioned, where *kurios* is the ground for the obligation to sing praise.[1] But the content expressed by the word *kurios* is also found in the N.T., quite apart from the actual word: the personal, legitimate, comprehensive sovereignty of God.

3. *Jesus the Lord*

It will be well to start with St. Paul, whose use of *kurios* is clear. The other N.T. writings will then be added in support and by way of clarification and as tokens of the consistency of usage.

[1] In the foregoing lines those passages have been selected in which *kurios*, used of God, has a special tone and could not be replaced by *theos* without altering the sense.

In I Cor. xii. 3, St. Paul contrasts *anathema Iēsous* with *kurios Iēsous*. The former is an expression of what Acts calls *blasphēmein*—to speak of Jesus as being opposed to God and so incur God's judgement. It is a strictly religious attitude, opposing something for the sake of God. A corresponding expression for its opposite is lacking: it would be *eulogētos*, but in the N.T. that is reserved for God. Thus *kurios Iēsous* is not exactly parallel to *anathema Iēsous*, as the latter predicate can be applied to much and many in some sense, but not the former. But in any case it includes a religious declaration for Jesus, " for the sake of God "; this attitude is only possible and legitimate towards One Person.

We are led further by the well-known, inexhaustible passage in Phil. ii. 6-11, especially verses 9-11: *dio kai ho theos auton huperhupsōsen kai echarisato autōi to onoma to huper pan onoma, hina en tōi onomati Iēsou pan gonu kampsēi . . . kai pāsa glōssa exomologēsetai hoti kurios Iēsous Christos eis dōxan theou patros.* The name, which the repetition of the article indicates to be a very special one, can only be the name of *kurios*. It has been given to Jesus as the divine answer (*dio*) to his mortal sufferings in obedience. At the name which Jesus, who took upon Himself the form of a slave, has received, i.e. in the presence of Him who was in history and has been raised on high, the whole world bows. So too Revelation (v. 12) says precisely of the *arnion hōs esphagmenon* that it is " worthy " to receive the book which comprises the liberation of mankind, to receive *dunamis*, *doxa* and *eulogia*. The name of *kurios* involves equality with God: the " bowing the knee " and the exclamation *kurios Iēsous Christos* belong together, and, although Philippians does not actually quote Isa. xlv. 23 f., the *exomologēsis*, especially in the LXX but also in the masoretic text, so runs that *kurios Iēsous Christos* does not link on to it, and yet there is a substitution of *en tōi onomati Iēsou* for *emoi* (sc. *kampsei pan gonu*) on the lips of God. But that this Jesus is acknowledged as *kurios* is to the glory of God. Thus the name of *kurios* comprises the exaltation. In the light of this there is no need to decide whether the *huper* in *huperupsōsen* relates to *en morphēi theou huparchōn*, or only means " beyond all measure ".

The whole N.T. uses *kurios* of Jesus as the resurrected. In Rom. x. 9, St. Paul expressly sets the confession of the lordship of Jesus side by side with the heart's faith that God has raised Him from the dead. Acts ii. 36 records St. Peter as saying at the end of the Pente-cost sermon: *asphalōs oun ginōsketō pās oikos Israēl hoti kai kurion auton kai Christon epoiēsen ho theos, touton ton Iēsoun hon hūmeis estaurōsate*. The larger the share of St. Luke in the formulation of this passage, the clearer is the indication of the connexion in his mind between the resurrection and the *kuriotēs* of Jesus. The connexion between the suffering, resurrection and the divine status of Jesus which is expressed by *kurios*, appears often, without the word *kurios* being specially prominent: thus when Heb. ii. 6 ff. quotes Ps. viii. 5 ff., it is in verse 8 that it is first shown that the text cannot relate merely to man but rather (verse 9) relates to Jesus, who is crowned with *doxa* and *timē* because of his death-pangs: in this the lordship of Jesus is already pointed to, without the author going so far as to say expressly that the *panta hupetaxas hupo-katō tōn podōn autou* has also been fulfilled in him. The same connexion between resurrection and lordship is also shown by the words of the Risen One in Matt. xxviii. 18: *edothē moi pāsa exousia en ouranōi kai epi gēs:* he who has *exousia* is *kurios*. Most clearly of all, however, is the connexion to be seen in the use of Ps. cx. 1. This passage is the sole basis for the idea of

8

sitting at the right hand of God. It occurs nowhere
else. But in this Psalm the sitting at the right of God
is bound up with a being lord, in the Psalm with being
David's lord. Acts ii. 36, lets St. Peter draw the
consequence from this verse of the Psalm for Jesus with
a "therefore". Sitting at the right hand of God
connotes reigning with Him,[1] i.e. divine status, as does
the mere sitting in the presence of God (Babylonian
Chagiga 15a; Hebrew *Enoch* xvi. 3).

The echoes of this Psalm passage in the N.T. mostly
show the connexion between resurrection and exaltation
(cf. also Acts v. 31; Rom. viii. 34; Col. iii. 1; Heb. i.
3, 13, viii. 1, xii. 2; Rev. iii. 21—cf. Rom. i. 4) and
between exaltation and universal lordship (cf. I Cor.
xv. 25 ff.—where Ps. viii. 7 is also used) similarly Eph. i.
20 f., also I Pet. iii. 22 and Heb. x. 12 f.).

In I Cor. xi. 3, St. Paul mentions a series of ranks:
*thelō de humas eidenai hoti pantos andros hē kephalē ho
Christos estin, kephalē de gunaikos ho anēr, kephalē de tou
Christou ho theos.* It is inconceivable that St. Paul means
that woman is further from Christ than man. The
whole passage deals with the natural superiority of man.
The universe, of which the relationship between man
and woman is a constituent, has no direct relationship
to God, but only one through Christ. Without Him,
the "world" could not exist before God. It is
through Christ that the world can exist before God,
it is He who exercises God's sovereignty towards the
world. As the heavenly, earthly and subterranean
powers bow their knees before Him (Phil. ii. 10) so
(in Col. ii. 10) He is *kephalē* (the same expression as in
I Cor. xi. 3) *pasēs archēs kai exousias*, He is *pro pantōn
kai ta panta en autōi sunestēken* (Col. i. 17), and with
reference to this cosmic [2] status of Christ in the foregoing

[1] Josephus, *Ant.* vi. 235.
[2] " Cosmic " here includes mankind.

verses Paul summarises (*oun*) by saying (Col. ii. 6)
hōs oun parelabete ton Christon Iēsoun ton kurion. . . . Here
kurios, with special emphasis on it (cf. the repeated
article) summarises all that Paul has told the Colossians
about Christ in the preceding sentences. That the
world as it is cannot subsist in the sight of God depends
upon its fallen nature; cf. Col. i. 20—*di' autou apokatal-
laxai ta panta eis auton, eirēnopoiēsas dia tou haimatos tou
staurou autou, di' autou eite ta epi tēs gēs eite ta en tois ouranois*;
cf. Eph. i. 20, f.; I Pet. iii. 22. The Son exercises
God's sovereignty over the world in order to lay it—
and with it Himself—at the Father's feet, after the
overcoming of all opposing forces (I Cor. xv. 28). The
lordship of Jesus, by which He exercises God's almighty
sway over the world, thus has as its goal the putting of
the reconciled and judged world in subjection to God.

In this process, however, the cardinal factor is mankind. Without detracting from the cosmic extent of His
lordship sketched above, its centre of gravity is His
lordship over men (Rom. xiv. 9—*eis touto gar Christos
apethanen kai ezēsen, hina kai nekrōn kai zōntōn kurieusēi*.
That is shown by the Pauline usage: [1] (*ho*) *Christos* is
He who died on the Cross and has risen again (Rom.
v. 6, 8, vi. 4, 9, xiv. 9; I Cor. i. 23 f., v. 7, viii. 11, xv. 3,
12 ff.; Gal. iii. 13, etc.);[2] the word appears when it is
a question of the work of redemption (Rom. viii. 35,
xv. 7; II Cor. iii. 14, v. 14, 18 f.; Gal. iii. 13); this
work is in evidence when Paul exhorts through the
praütēs kai epieikeia tou Christou (II Cor. x. 1, cf. I Cor.
xi. 1). It is called *to euangellion tou Christou* (Rom. xv.
19; I Cor. ix. 12; II Cor. ii. 12, iv. 4, ix. 13, x. 14;

[1] Cf. the works of Stead, Burton and Dobschütz in the Bibliography ; also H. E. Weber, in *Neue kirchliche Zeitschrift* xxxi
(1920), pp. 254-8.
[2] For what follows, cf. the tables in Foerster, *Herr ist Jesus*,
pp. 237 ff.

Gal. i. 7, cf. I Cor. i. 6; II Cor. iii. 3) being crucified, dead, with " Christ " (Rom. vi. 8, vii. 4; Gal. ii. 19) baptised into Him (Gal. iii. 27). " Christ " has called the Galatians into grace (Gal. i. 6), with the fullness of the blessing (*eulogia*) of " Christ " Paul is certain of coming to Rome (Rom. xv. 29), " Christ " has sent him (I Cor. i. 17; Rom. xvi. 9; I Cor. iv. 1; Gal. i. 10; II Cor. xi. 13, 23; the community is one body " in Christ ", Rom. xii. 5; Gal. i. 22).

On the other hand, *kurios* looks towards the exalted Lord who is authority (I Cor. iv. 19, xiv. 37, xvi. 7— cf. Jas. iv. 15): it is the " lord " whom the faithful serve (Rom. xii. 11; I Cor. xii.5; Eph. vi. 7; Col. iii. 23). Everyone stands or falls with his " lord " (Rom. xiv. 4-8, cf. I Cor. vii. 32-5, Rom. xvi. 12, 22, II Cor. viii. 5); that is also true of private life (I Cor. vii. 39). Actions must be worthy of the " lord " (I Cor. xi. 27; Rom. xvi. 2). It is the exalted Lord who dispenses to each one the measure of his faith (I Cor. iii. 5, vii. 17). It is the " lord " who is coming (I Thess. iv. 15 ff.; I Cor. iv. 5, xi. 26; Phil. iv. 5) and who is the judge (I Thess. iv. 6; II Thess. i. 9; I Cor. iv. 4, xi. 32; II Cor. v. 11, x. 18). In this life Paul sojourns " away from " the " lord " (II Cor. v. 6 ff.). He is the lord of His servants, to whom He gives full authority (II Cor. x. 8, xiii. 10) at whose work the community members remain steadfast (I Cor. xv. 58) as, e.g. Timothy (I Cor. iv. 17, xvi. 10). Paul's " work in the lord " is the church at Corinth (I Cor. ix. 1-2); in Troy Paul found a door opened " in the lord " (II Cor. ii. 12). He is the one lord of all (Rom. x. 12), " Christ " is proclaimed as " lord " (II Cor. iv. 5). This exalted " lord " is the Spirit (II Cor. iii. 9) it is to " the Lord " that Paul prays for release from his sufferings (II Cor. xii. 8). The summary of all this is found in I Cor. viii. 5 f.: *eiper eisin legomenoi theoi* . . .

*all' hēmin heis theos ho patēr . . . kai heis kurios Iēsous
Christos, di' hou to panta kai hēmeis di' autou.* " There
are many so-called gods in heaven and earth "—here
Paul is thinking of the fact that rulers too are equated
with gods. In fact, he adds, there are (more than
those who speak of gods in Heaven and on earth are
aware of) many gods (cf. Phil. iii. 19—*hōn ho theos hē
koilia*) and many " lords "—much upon which men are
dependent, and that consists of real powers. Thus
Paul makes no distinction between *theos* and *kurios* in
the sense that *kurios* denotes a mediator-divinity: there
are no instances of this in the environment of primitive
Christianity.[1] *Kurios* is here a term expressing relationship, it denotes that upon which men make themselves dependent or are in fact dependent. For the
Christians there is only one God with whom they have
to reckon, from and to whom all things exist (cf.
I Cor. xv. 28, p. 101, lines 10 ff *supra*), and only one
Lord upon whom they depend, to whom they owe
everything that makes them Christian. Here again it
is clear that *kurios* means He through whom God has
interposed into this world to save and to act.

Thus it is not the case that the distinction between
Christos and *kurios* is drawn according to some fixed
scheme. *Eis Christon hamartanete* (not *eis ton kurion*)
says Paul (I Cor. viii. 12) and thereby wishes to make
clear to the Corinthians that by their thoughtless
behaviour they are sinning against Him who died for

[1] Even Bousset, op. cit. p. 99, is obliged to supplement his contention that " while the Apostle, using the concept of *kyrios*, on the one
side places his Lord at the very side of God and yet also subor-
dinates Him in a certain manner, he thought there were analogies
for this differentiation within the Godhead in hellenistic religion ",
with his second note that it is not quite clear " what the Apostle
must have been thinking of when he presupposes that the difference of meaning between the words *theos* and *kurios* was well-
known ".

them and the brethren. It is the same with Rom.
xiv. 18: *ho . . . en toutōi douleuōn tōi Christōi.* On the
other hand, I Cor. xi. 26 has *ton thanaton tou kuriou
katangellete,* in contrast to the common usage, perhaps
because *achri hou elthēi* follows. In I Cor. vii. 22,
Paul, presumably upon grounds of style, changes the
expression: *ho gar en kuriōi klētheis doulos apeleutheros
kuriou estin* with *homoiōs ho eleutheros klētheis doulos estin
Christou.*

Besides the use of the simple *kurios,* or *(Iēsous)
Christos,* we find also varying conjunctions of the two.
Here too one has to reckon with a certain amount of
freedom of usage. The fact that 10 out of the 27 Pauline
uses of *ho kurios (hēmōn) Iēsous,* without *Christos,* are in
Thessalonians and 14 of the 18 non-Pauline uses are in
Acts is doubtless due to the youth of the Church in
Thessalonica and the missionary character of Acts.
The variation *ho kurios (hēmōn) Iēsous (Christos)* occurs
besides the simple *(Iēsous) Christos* or *kurios.* In Gal.
vi. 14 we find *kauchasthai . . . en tōi staurōi tou kuriou
hēmōn Iēsou Christou* alongside the numerous cases in
which, in this context, *Christos* stands alone, similarly,
e.g. Eph. iii. 11; Rom. v. 1, vi. 23, viii. 39; I Cor. xv.
57; I Thess. v. 9; and in contexts in which *ho kurios*
otherwise stands alone, the more detailed variation
occurs in Rom. xv. 30, xvi. 18; I Cor. i. 7, 8, 10; II Cor.
i. 14; I Thess. ii. 15, 19, iii. 13, iv. 2, v. 23; II Thess.
ii. 1; I Tim. vi. 14. It is clearly noticeable how the
longer form of the name of Jesus expresses a certain
emphasis and solemnity; so especially in the initial and
final greetings and decisive phases of the thought—
Rom. v. 1, viii. 39; I Cor. xv. 57; Rom. xv. 30. A
further element is introduced by the addition of a
personal pronoun, usually *hēmōn,* to *kurios.* The
general meaning is made clear by Phil. iii. 8—*hēgoumai
panta zēmian einai dia to huperechon tēs gnōseōs Christou Iesou*

tou kuriou mou—that of a personal allegiance. But it must be emphasised that it is not the allegiance of a lazy slave to his lord or between every slave and even the harshest master, whom his slave inwardly despises. The *hēmōn* in *ho kurios hēmōn Iēsous Christos* does not indicate a mere coupling together. " I never knew you " is the Lord's answer to " many " (Matt. vii. 23). Paul calls Him *Christos Iēsous ho kurios mou* (cf. Rev. xi. 8), because he is privileged to call Him his Lord, because He is the Lord who is for him, who " regards him as loyal " (I Tim. i. 12). The " our " which is always otherwise used refers to all Christians, not a single church, just as " your Lord Jesus Christ " never occurs. Christendom owes all that it is and has to the fact that it is " His " and He " its Lord ". Therefore it may be that with the " our " another element comes in, that of the sense of belonging to-gether of the congregations which imposes obligations (Rom. xv. 30: *parakalō de humās dia tou kuriou hēmōn Iēsou Christou . . . sunagōnisasthai moi en tais proseuchais huper emou*—cf. I Cor. i. 10), which binds together (I Cor. i. 2), but which also separates them from others (Rom. xvi. 18: *hoi gar toioutoi tōi kuriōi hēmōn Christōi ou douleuousin*).

(*b*) In the N.T. Epistles and in Acts *kurios* is also used in a sense which we have not yet discussed, namely, for the " historical Jesus ": " I charge, not I, but *ho kurios* " (I Cor. vii. 10)—with these words Paul refers to a " word of the Lord ". Similarly in I Cor. ix. 14 and vii. 25, Paul says, in reference to the lack of any definite word of the Lord over this question *epitagēn kuriou ouch echō*. The same situation is behind I Cor. vii. 12—*legō egō, ouch ho kurios*. In I Thess. iv. 16, *touto gar humin legomen en logōi kuriou*, Paul is probably referring to a saying of Jesus which has not come down to us. Although in this passage one might think that *kurios* was used to denote authority, this point of view does not fit Gal. i. 19, nor I Cor. ix. 5—James the brother, and the brothers, *tou kuriou*. It is also the historical Lord who is in mind in Heb. ii. 3: (*sōtēria*) *hētis archēn labousa laleisthai dia tou kuriou hupo tōn akousantōn eis hēmas ebaiōthē*. An unrecorded word of the Lord is reckoned by Paul as one of the *logoi tou kuriou Iēsou* in Acts xx. 35: a recorded one is introduced in Acts xi. 16 with *emnēsthēn de tou rhēmatos tou kuriou*. This usage is also once paralleled in the gospels. Luke uses *ho kurios* thirteen times [1] always in L or in independent formulations, while John uses it similarly five times.[2] Otherwise *kurios* is only used in the gospels, except in the vocative, by Jesus in Mark xi. 3, par.: *kai ean tis humin eipēi: ti poieite touto? eipate: ho kurios autou chreian echei*, and, on the lips of Peter, in John xxi. 7: *ho kurios estin*. True, in Mark xi. 3, it is not quite clear whether in the Aramaic, in which " lord " is bound to have some suffix, the disciples must have said " our ", " thy " or " his " (the donkey's) lord, or whether (cf. Mark v. 19) *ho kurios* is here a designation of God. The parallel with Mark xiv. 14, makes it probable that an " our ", referring to the disciples, was linked as suffix to the original Aramaic word.

Modes of addressing Jesus demand separate treatment. In Mark it is only the Syropheonician woman who uses *kurie* (vii. 28), the disciples, Pharisees and people use *didaskale*.[3] Matthew has kept *didaskale* in Markan material only on the lips of Pharisees and Judas Iscariot and in ambiguous cases, and otherwise replaces it by *kurie*: thus for him *didaskale* as a mode

[1] vii. 13, 19, x. 1, 39, 41, xi. 39, xiii. 15, xvii. 5, 6, xviii. 6, xix. 8, xxii. 61 (twice); xvi. 8 and xxiv. 34 are omitted.

[2] iv. 1, vi. 23, xi. 2, xx. 2, 13, not counting xx. 18, 20, 25, xxi. 12, i.e. the passages which refer to the risen Lord.

[3] See Foerster, op. cit. pp. 216 ff.

of address connotes a definite reserve towards Jesus. Luke has kept *didaskale* in Markan material, or replaced it by *epistata*. In non-Markan passages he often has *kurie*, especially on the disciples' lips. In John *kurie* predominates. Mark and John have preserved original terms of address in *rhabbi* (Mark ix. 5, xi. 21, xiv. 45 (= Matt. xxvi. 49); John i. 38, 49, iii. 2, iv. 31, vi. 25, ix. 2, xi. 8 (and, in addressing the Baptist, John iii. 26)), and *rhabbouni* (Mark x. 51, John xx. 16). Both these are specifically translated as *didaskale* by John. Luke (always) and Matthew (generally) have reproduced this alien word by *kurie* (Matthew, Luke, e.g. xviii. 41 for *rhabbouni*) and *epistata*. In an unparalleled passage, Matthew xxvi. 25, Judas addresses Jesus as *rhabbi*. As to the meaning of this term, Mark and John must be regarded as its oldest and best interpreters. Even the independent Lukan translation (*epistata*) shows that a difference was felt between *rabbî* and *mârî*.

Thus in Mark Jesus is only once addressed as *kurie*, by a gentile woman, otherwise He is spoken to as *rhabbi* (only, of course, when some term of address is employed). The latter term has the sense of an address of honour, used especially to those learned in the law. The less frequent *rhabbouni* is closer to *mârî*, although John treats it as identical with *rabbi*. Luke reproduces it by *kurie*. It is unlikely that we ought to attach so much importance to the Marcan tradition as to conclude that Jesus was never addressed as *mârî*. For in Luke vi. 46; Matt. vii. 21 f., xxv. 11, the duplication of *kurie* is semitic—why not then the word as well? Moreover, in John xiii. 13, Jesus expressly refers to both the appellations *ho didaskalos* and *ho kurios*, and *mârî* is not impossible as a title used in addressing a scholar,[1] and was more common than *rabbî* as a mode

[1] Jer. Talmud, *Ketubboth*, 28d, l. 43. Dalman, op. cit. p. 267.

of address in general. That *mârî* is not mentioned in
Matt. xxiii. 7 ff. among the titles which Jesus forbids
to the disciples is bound up with the fact that the title
of rabbi was given to persons who had in any case no
right to it.

Didaskalos is also the word used to describe the relationship of Jesus to His disciples by Himself and by others:
by Jesus Himself Mark xiv. 14, par.; Matt. x. 24 f.
par, (xxiii. 8), cf. John xiii. 14; by others in Mark only
v. 35, par., also Matt. ix. 11, xvii. 24; John iii. 2, xi. 28.
Thus to a considerable extent Jesus was not addressed
as " lord " during His sojourn on earth, nor referred
to as such.

But this supplies the germ for the later usage of
referring to the historical Jesus as the *kurios*. The
designation of the members of the family of Jesus as
desposunoi (Eusebius, *Hist. Eccl.* i. 7, 14) harks back in
its style to Palestine. Here is no transmutation into
another species, but a heightening of the style found in
the Gospels. That it was later, in Luke's special
material and in John, that the possibility emerged of
referring to Jesus as the *kurios*, is linked with the fact
that the formulation of the Gospel material is influenced
by the needs of evangelism.[1]

This *kurios*, however, must be sharply distinguished
from that which confronts us in the Epistles. It may
perhaps be inferred from the speeches in Acts that the
name of Lord was not immediately used for the
Ascended (against this are Acts ii. 36 and x. 36: but
according to iii. 20, the name of Messiah was at first
prevalent). It is important to look not for the origin,
but for the roots, of the use of *kurios* most clearly observ-
able in Paul. Most decisive is the resurrection of
Jesus. Without it the disciples, looking back upon
their relationship with Jesus, might at any moment

[1] Foerster, op. cit. pp. 213 ff.

have described it by saying that He had been their
Lord: but in fact it was a question of His being so
still. The relationship of personal ties to Jesus which
had characterised the dealings of the disciples with Him
was now through the resurrection vitally renewed and
sealed. The parables which describe the relationship
of Jesus to His disciples under the guise of a lord and
his slaves or servants now received their profoundest
significance; now the disciples were the servants
waiting for their lord. Since the disciples knew Jesus
to be at the right hand of God, their relationship to
Him now transcended all human analogies and became
purely religious, i.e. founded upon faith. A further
root which produced the use of Lord as a name for
Jesus is the use which Jesus twice made of Ps. cx—Mark
xii. 35 ff. par. and xiv. 62, par.[1] We have seen how
strong was the effect of this psalm upon the N.T. (cf.
supra, pp. 99-100, ff.). He who is David's lord is
thereby also Israel's lord, and, in the faith of the early
Church, lord of the New Israel. Perhaps the Palestinian original congregation went no further than that
—for them " lord " had always a genitive or personal
pronoun attached to it, " our lord " was there the
name for Jesus. That is also indicated by the Aramaic
word *maranatha*, which occurs twice in early Christianity—I Cor. xvi. 22 and the *Didache* x. 6. The
interpretation is disputed, whether it should be transcribed as *mâran 'ᵃthâ'*, or *mârana' thâ'*.[2] In any case the
phrase is about " our lord " and it refers to Jesus.
There is no ground for maintaining that the word did
not originate with the Palestinian church, since all the
Aramaic words preserved in the gospels did so and the
retention of the foreign-sounding words is only significant

---

[1] See also E. Meyer, *Ursprung und Anfänge des Christentums*, iii,
p. 218, n. 1.

[2] See E. Peterson. *Εἶς θεός* (1926), pp. 130 f.

if it derives from the first Christians and not from
some Aramaic-speaking congregation in Syria. In the
Greek-speaking congregations the personal pronoun
hēmōn, corresponding to the suffix, dropped off, as we
observed in the case with the gentile use of *kurios* for
gods (p. 27, lines 8 ff.). Thus *kurios*, used absolutely,
could express the comprehensive lordship of Jesus,
testifying that " the Father has given all judgment to
the Son " (John v. 22) and that to Him all authority
in Heaven and earth has been given (Matt. xxviii. 18).
If *kurios* expressed this, then the LXX passages which
mention *kurios* could be interpreted of Jesus: in Him
God acts in such a way as is said in the O.T. of the
kurios.

4. *Earthly Kurios-relationships*

In the N.T. a new look is given to earthly relationships of rank. This is clear from the relationship of
slaves to their masters: " Slaves, be subservient in all
respects to your *kurioi* in the flesh, not in *ophthalmodou-
liais*, as men-pleasers, but in singleness of heart, fearing
ton kurion. Whatever you do, work with your whole
soul as *tōi kuriōi* and not for men, knowing that you
will receive the reward of your inheritance *apo kuriou* "
(Col. iii. 22). It is a question of complete submission
to their lord, which also shuns *ophthalmodoulia*, superficial appearances of service, and is thus complete
loyalty. But this loyalty is only possible because
their service for their lords is their service of the
Lord, their service of God: thereby they can serve
their lords completely in their loyalty to Christ, free
from all human constraint. This focuses at one point
in relationships of rank the fundamental solution of
the whole problem raised by the word " lord ", a
problem which every people has sought to solve in its
own way.

1. INDEX OF WORDS AND REFERENCES

9

V. Apocrypha, etc.

VI. Rabbinic

GENERAL INDEX

(See also the Bibliography pp. ix – x)